A Storyteller

A Storyteller

*Mario Vargas Llosa between
Civilization and Barbarism*

Braulio Muñoz

ROWMAN & LITTLEFIELD PUBLISHERS, INC.
Lanham • Boulder • New York • Oxford

ROWMAN & LITTLEFIELD PUBLISHERS, INC.

Published in the United States of America
by Rowman & Littlefield Publishers, Inc.
4720 Boston Way, Lanham, Maryland 20706
http://www.rowmanlittlefield.com

12 Hid's Copse Road
Cumnor Hill, Oxford OX2 9JJ, England

British Cataloging in Publication Information Available

Library of Congress Cataloging-in-Publication Data
Muñoz, Braulio, 1946–
    A storyteller : Mario Vargas Llosa between civilization and
barbarism / Braulio Muñoz.
        p.   cm.
    Includes bibliographical references and index.
    ISBN 0-8476-9750-9 (cloth : alk. paper).—ISBN 0-8476-9751-7
(pbk. : alk. paper)
1. Vargas Llosa, Mario, 1936– —Criticism and interpretation.
I. Title.
II. PQ8498.32.A65Z77 2000
    863—dc21   99-38922
                                                            CIP

Printed in the United States of America

♾™ The paper used in this publication meets the minimum requirements of American
National Standard for Information Sciences—Permanence of Paper for Printed Library
Materials, ANSI Z.39.48–1992.

For Kevin and Michèle

Contents

Preface

There is a sense of roundedness in the interpretations of an author's canon. It is as if the overview of a lifetime effort makes possible the closing of the interpretive circle. This is why interpretations of the works of long-dead authors have an air of finality about them. In truth, all interpretations are provisory. Such is the hermeneutic horizon where humans and their words exist. This is clearest when the proffered interpretations deal with the canon of someone who, like Mario Vargas Llosa, is still writing. All interpretive works then bear the implicit qualifier: "so far."

As an urbanite upper-class Peruvian of the midcentury, Mario Vargas Llosa wishes us to acknowledge that he belongs squarely in the Western tradition. Perhaps more than most Peruvian intellectuals of his generation, he has displayed a strong determination to follow in the footsteps of such theorists as Karl Marx and Karl Popper and writers such as Flaubert and Faulkner. The long and arduous labor appears to have secured him a place in that tradition. It is quite proper, therefore, that his lifework be examined in all its overdetermined Western dimensions.

The following reflections are not meant to provide an exhaustive treatment of these dimensions. The relationship between Vargas Llosa's canon and the Western tradition is too complex to be captured in all its nuances here. Rather, these reflections focus on Vargas Llosa's treatment of key aspects of the Western socio-theoretical tradition, such as the long-standing debates regarding the antinomy of the Individual and Society, while listening for resonances that might help us understand the successful weaving of literature and social theory by one of Latin America's most influential cultural leaders.

To grasp the animus of Vargas Llosa's work one must begin by paying close attention to his own discourse. Unlike many Latin American writer/critics, Vargas Llosa is exceedingly and publicly self-conscious about his life and work. He has bared his soul for years, and he expects to be taken at his word. But if our own reflections are to avoid redundancy, they must lead us one step further. They must touch on the psychocultural sediment underlying the public confessions. For authors are not always the best judges of their creations; they often are too harsh or too forgiving. The reflections offered here are meant as extensions of Mario Vargas Llosa's own ruminations.

Two aspects of the underlying psychocultural sediment are worth anticipating here. First, precisely because of his recurrent jeremiads against his people and culture, which at times border on self-hatred, Vargas Llosa must be counted among the clearest exemplars of Mestizo Man: an embattled being who embodies the fundamental contradictions of our times. Second, the weight of the psychocultural sediment explains in large part why Mario Vargas Llosa must be seen at once as a truncated Lawgiver and a gifted Storyteller.

Acknowledgments

In February 1998 several friends gathered to discuss an earlier version of this work. Thank you Gustavo Benavides, Hugh Lacey, Richard Eldridge, John Hassett, and Nancy K. Muñoz. During his senior year at Swarthmore College, Aaron Ross was an insightful interlocutor concerning neoliberal economics. Thank you, Aaron. And thank you again, Nancy, for your endless patience and wonderful sense of humor.

1

On Literature

The land of literature is a fairy land to those who view it at a distance, but, like all other landscapes, the charm fades on a nearer approach, and the thorns and briars become visible.

—W. Irving

ART AND SOCIETY

The place that the offerings of the artistic vision occupy in the Western cultural tradition, particularly with regard to the conceptions of the Good Life, has always been at once vague and precarious. During the period of Athenian democracy the artistic vision flourished; but Plato banished artists from his Republic. During the Enlightenment, following Kant, Schiller held that the task of art is to educate humanity; but Hegel argued that art had been superceded by philosophy as the clearest statement about the designs of God in history. In the afterglow of the Enlightenment, art was seen as a handmaiden to politics—by the right and the left. Then, almost as a last gasp, artists and critics asserted art as self-sufficient: *l'art pour l'art*. The retreat into pure form was apparently unsuccessful. There are those today who claim that the aesthetic daemon, as God, is dead.[1]

Within this problematic position of art in Western culture, literature offers an even more precarious case. For centuries it trailed behind the other arts in being regarded as an adequate vehicle for offering enduring insights into the human condition, even among those willing and able to appreciate the artistic temperament. No doubt the suspicion endured largely because of literature's close proximity to the populace, the everyday, the temporal, and hence, the ephemeral.

1

Poetry gained reluctant acceptance as a proper vehicle to talk about the Good
Life in large measure because it claimed to have overcome the weight of time
and to have grasped veritable essences. The case for the novel—produced for
mass consumption—as a proper form of artistic expression was still being
assessed by the middle of this century.[2]

ON THE PERIPHERY

It is self-evident that questions concerning the Good Life are, necessarily, ethical
questions. Therefore, they must engage ongoing political and economic debates.
Furthermore, given Europe's political and economic ascendancy in world history,
particularly since the fifteenth century, it was inevitable that the controversies
regarding artistic visions of the Good Life would ricochet, not only within but
also beyond the European cultural borders. In effect, ever since then, an increasing sector of humanity—those inhabiting the so-called third-world countries—
have been deeply affected by debates in which they did not participate. Once their
traditional notions of Beauty or Truth had been undermined by an aggressive
European animus, the discussions concerning the Good Life were carried out
under the watchful eyes of colonial centers of power. As a consequence, the ethical dimensions of art dispersed as echoes of faraway realities. This was certainly
true in the case of Latin America; at least until the middle of this century.

VARGAS LLOSA: LITERATURE AS PROTEST

Within the Latin American tradition, conceived as an extension of the Western
world, the Peruvian writer/critic Mario Vargas Llosa (1936–) must be considered among those who have most vociferously argued for embracing literature in
general and the novel in particular, as proper vehicles for saying something
meaningful about the Good Life. What are Vargas Llosa's reasons for making the
claim? Why should we accept his proposition?

From very early on, Vargas Llosa has conceived literature—the act of writing
it and secondarily the act of reading it—as a form of protest. With nuanced extensions and restrictions, he has retained this initial appraisal. In a general sense, he
posits, literature translates humanity's protest against the finitude, the bounded-
ness, of its condition. It expresses a discontentment with our limitations as perceived against the free play of our imagination. Through the act of writing—and
of reading—we make light of the heavy chains of the mundane. In other words,
following in the footsteps of Georg Lukacs and Walter Benjamin, Vargas Llosa
posits that literature always says "and yet" to life. In a more particular sense, Vargas Llosa holds that literature is also a protest against the concrete evils of the
writer's reality. These concrete evils provide the occasion for the creative act;

they are the necessary instantiations of a general condition. Without a protesting animus, both against life itself and against its evil instantiations, the literary act is impossible.[3]

In protesting against the limits of the human condition, holds Vargas Llosa, literature expands our horizons. In its innermost core, the literary vision strives to express the manifoldness of the human experience, and hence to teach us something essential about ourselves: that we all have a share in the common, temporal project; that history is the trail of our common hope. In disclosing for us this essential Truth, the literary vision overflows all limitations.

GOOD AND EVIL

In principle, the guiding animus of literature is to examine the Good as well as the Evil side of our humanity. Therefore, the overflowing of boundaries cannot be seen as an inevitable movement toward the Sublime. Early in his career, Vargas Llosa followed George Bataille rather closely. Literature, he argued, expresses best the Evil side of the human condition. This meant the writer experiences, examines, and discloses that which the rest of us would rather keep from view. There was more: it was not only that literature provides the occasion for reflection on such Evil reality. Literature, Vargas Llosa argued then, sustains, defends, even admires, the Evil side of humanity. And yet, it is important to note that, even in the moments when he was closest to Bataille, Vargas Llosa managed to put some distance between them. While agreeing that literature must often begin from the Evil side, he also noted that, when seen in its proper dimensions, literature is most profound when it strives to speak about the totality of human experience.[4]

The need for such a corrective is self-evident. The literary act is more than a vehicle for the release of pent-up resentment, forbidden desires, or hidden daemons. The artistic vision strains to offer us glimpses of the Good Life as well. This position was more thoroughly developed by Vargas Llosa later in his career. But, of course, the matter is even more complicated than that. The very premises of Bataille's offerings and Vargas Llosa's corrective stand in need of reflection. How are we to understand what is Evil and what is Good in any given society, never mind Humanity?

CONTINGENCIES

From the standpoint of much current social theorizing, if we bracket out the larger question and talk only about Western societies (we must neutralize the necessary nuances of even that complex, of course), the only way to make sense of this conception of literature is by assuming that it expresses what is considered

Good or Evil by the "normal" society that gives it ground. In this case, what is Good or Evil would not be defined by the literary vision itself, but by the society of which it is a part. The "and yet" of literature would then be grounded not in its own insights regarding Good and Evil, but in an already established conception of the Good Life. The pugilistic stance Vargas Llosa wishes to assign to literature would then become contrariness. The conception of art as a particular kind of knowing, something Kant had celebrated, would be left behind.

Let us take a closer look. Since at least the nineteenth century—under the impact of the lifetime efforts by such founders of modern social theory as Marx, Nietzsche, Weber, Freud, and Durkheim—it has become a truism in the Western sociotheoretical tradition that not only the conception of Good and Evil but also Good and Evil themselves are historically contingent. No modern Western intellectual can now speak for Evil without, at the same time, questioning his or her own position; because the possibility of choosing to stand above Good and Evil in order to then take sides is given only with the undermining of all truth-claims. One person's Evil is always someone else's Good. Hence, taking the side of Evil, or letting Evil speak—through literature—could be equally, and perhaps more correctly, understood as speaking for a particular conception of Good.

In general terms, Vargas Llosa agrees with the main representatives of the Western sociotheoretical tradition. He accepts that what he might consider Evil in Peruvian society—as a concrete manifestation of Evil in general—might well be seen as a Good by other Peruvians. There is a strong relativist component in his aesthetic and critical production. However (and here we encounter an instance of an oscillation that is endemic to his work), he does not wish to fall prey to the paralyzing embrace of relativism. Against the insights of Western social theory, he wishes to hold that literature discloses some Truth. In other words, Vargas Llosa embraces Kant's notion of the aesthetic as a way of knowing.

Furthermore, he attempts to overcome the relativism entailed in the modern discourse of Good and Evil by insisting that a writer ought not be interested in taking sides. Echoing Max Weber's famous injunction, he holds that an artist can embrace the aesthetic daemon fully; that it alone ought to hold the fibers of his very life.[5] Vargas Llosa believes, as did Weber, that objectivity can be attained by the sheer weight of honest commitment. But, of course, the hope nestled in the claim is highly debatable, to say the least.

VIRILE MATURITY

The stance above Good and Evil presupposes a writer willing and able to face the world devoid of illusions; perhaps to show what Georg Lukacs called "virile maturity." A difficult posture to maintain, surely. But Vargas Llosa does not believe it impossible; the writer can indeed approximate an olympic figure. Contemplating the chaos that is human existence, the writer can attempt to provide order, if only in his imagined world. Contemplating a stifling existing order, the writer can attempt to portray mystery, playfulness, or absurdity. In other words, the writer can both introduce a skeptical standpoint, which helps to break the spell of the norm, and provide glimpses of a better world. It is in this context that the full extent of Vargas Llosa's notion of the *elemento añadido* (added element) in literature can be appreciated. In his offerings, the writer intends an imaginative reconstruction of reality. In and through his art, argues Vargas Llosa, leaving Kant's pietistic modesty behind, the writer competes with God: he aims at rectifying His creation.[6]

Needless to say, we postmodern intellectuals need convincing that the writer is capable of approaching an olympic figure. Minimally, we would have to be shown that the notion of "genius," that mischievous Western cultural valuation, conveys adequately whatever it is that makes possible the privileged standpoint of the artist as someone-who-knows. For there is no question that Vargas Llosa's conception of the writer harks back to the Kantian conception of genius, which lingered for decades in the hollow halls of the Western academy. It seems as though it only appeared that, under the impact of modernity, such a conception of the artist had withered away, together with the social substratum that made it possible. Since Vargas Llosa claims the writer is a supplanter of God, it behooves us to listen. A resurrection might be in the offing.

ELEMENTOS AÑADIDOS AND THE NOVEL

In his philosophical essay on the novel form, Georg Lukacs reiterates an idea that had been formulated with regard to bourgeois art more generally: the rise of the genre is deeply connected with the development of capitalism and the attendant modernity in the West. Therefore, the most recent literary formation is the epic of a world abandoned by God; it is the manifestation of radical skepticism. This is so, to paraphrase Octavio Paz, because the novel functions as an acid that corrodes the social world; it questions the reality of reality and embraces the utter relativity of Good and Evil. As we have seen, Vargas Llosa concurs.[7] At the same time, he oscillates. In a world abandoned by God, and therefore bereft of asymptotes for leading the Good Life, Vargas Llosa holds, the writer of novels feels an inner compulsion to "improve" on reality by offering Truth. In other words, against Lukacs's caution, Vargas Llosa believes the writer must take upon his shoulders the burden of providing a more rounded and integrated world.

The literary corrective to the world of God can be seen on two levels: first, as an effective supplantation of God in the fictive world. That is, in literature, the writer can create a world taking into account humanity's historically developed imaginings and desires. In this sense, literature aims to reiterate the old view of the aesthetic as a protest against the finitude of existence. But Vargas Llosa often writes and behaves as if the deicidal deed aims further. As an artist, he claims, the writer has something important to say about the "real" world as well. On this second level, the corrective act consists in adding something to reality that the artist either perceives as missing or intuits as repressed. In fact, the success of the deed can be taken as a marker for the distinction between great and lesser works. The *elemento añadido* is the Truth offered by aesthetics.

SOURCES

The *elemento añadido*, the aesthetic contribution over against God, Vargas Llosa claims, might issue from a variety of sources: psychological, biological, or mystical, which might be felt as resentment, nostalgia, rage, or despair.[8] From his extant writing, it is difficult to ascertain exact sources. What is clear is that the aesthetic Truth is not necessarily grounded on Reason. Its claim to universality rests on its power to tap the sediment of memories and feelings that humanity has achieved in its long trajectory over time. *Elementos añadidos* are akin to Kantian synthetic judgments.

In the Western world, where the achievements of science tend to smother all ways of knowing save the scientific method, this *elemento añadido* seems to give the novel an independence that permits it to tap into alternative ways of knowing and being. This is the main reason why the novel for Vargas Llosa could never be supplanted by anthropology, sociology, or psychology. The *elemento añadido* is the contribution of an artist's originality and creativity. The originality and creativity of an author, therefore, ought not to be judged only in terms of technical prowess or the felicitous use of language. The function of technique is to enhance the possibilities of the *elemento añadido*.[9]

ELEMENTOS AÑADIDOS AND LITERARY INDEPENDENCE

It is well known that writers of the Latin American "boom"—Carlos Fuentes, Julio Cortázar, José Donoso, García Márquez, in addition to Vargas Llosa himself—wished to distance themselves from their nineteenth-century predecessors, who they believed had labored under misguided approaches to art (such as regionalism, parochial versions of naturalism and romanticism, Indigenismo, and social realism). In the context of art as a way of knowing, Vargas Llosa wishes to call attention to one particular shortcoming: the tradition of writers such as Círo Alegría and Rómulo Gallegos was much too content to borrow not only the form and content of their creations from Europeans, but the *elementos añadidos* as well. In other words, mimesis took the place of originality and creativity. This is the main reason why artistic works from Latin America prior to the midcentury rang hollow.

(It is interesting to note that in order to contribute his own *elementos añadidos* to the Latin American—and the world—literary tradition, Vargas Llosa had to become more and more European; that he gained his originality by immersing himself in the tradition his predecessors had, according to him, merely copied. This immanent project, which demanded that he risk losing himself in order to know himself, has scarred the long trajectory of his love-hate relationship with Peru and Latin America. The trajectory reached a precarious resting place a few years ago when he became a Spaniard.)

LITERATURE AND FREEDOM

Gustave Flaubert was a likable bourgeois and an unlikely rebel. And yet, Vargas Llosa points out, it is precisely he who, through his art, has endured in the Western tradition as an incisive critic of his times. Following Flaubert, Vargas Llosa also believes that great literature will always be dangerous to the powers that be. This is the reason why such powers—state, party, religion, and the Many—will always try to control it. The threat to literature was greater in the past, he thinks, when societies had not progressed enough. For history shows that the high valuation of a free imagination is a good indicator of the level of civilization a society has attained. All mature societies tolerate an active imagination; they find it a necessary risk—the price of freedom.[10]

Vargas Llosa means to defend an artistic vision, not the animus of a political track. Within his Latin American tradition, he faults Indigenismo and social realism for compromising the artistic vision in view of political aims. The aesthetic critique of reality, he reiterates, is not necessarily consciously undertaken. On the contrary, the most fruitful and radical insights into alternative value systems offered by aesthetics issue from the unconscious play of the imagination. This was certainly the case with Flaubert, whose creative genius produced insights that were at odds with his consciously held sociopolitical interests. His insights into the havoc caused by the rise of capitalism are deftly woven in his art. When the author is given to preaching a consciously held political position, Vargas Llosa holds, he courts falling prey to a paternalistic and totalitarian animus.[11] Art demands absolute devotion.

OSCILLATIONS

We have encountered here the first instances of Vargas Llosa's oscillation between relativism and universalism. On the one hand, he refuses to draw the logical conclusion of the Western sociotheoretical tradition—deftly demonstrated by postmodernist writers such as Foucault, Derrida, and Lacan—and embrace relativism. On the other, he ignores the erosion of the grounding values of this tradition (Logos, Dialectic, Science) and holds fast to universalist values. In other words, Vargas Llosa wishes to have it both ways. Social theorists such as Marx or Freud got away with this oscillation because at the core of their theories they retained untheorized positive values from the Western tradition, such as Justice and Freedom. In a postmodern world, such valuations are no longer taken for granted; they stand in need of justification. These days, even within the ongoing Western sociotheoretical tradition, a return to the nineteenth-century stance is considered either naive or disingenuous. The Kantian notion of genius is no longer enough.

2

Daemons and the Total Novel

The novel is the art-form of virile maturity: this means that the completeness of the novel's world, if seen objectively, is an imperfection, and if subjectively experienced, it amounts to resignation.

—G. Lukacs

DAEMONS

According to Plato, Socrates was beholden to his daemon; he was not free to ignore the call deep within his soul and intellect. At length, of course, to listen meant for Socrates to drink his hemlock. Even in the end, however, the wisest man in Athens strove to have it both ways: to obey his daemon and carry on with the maeutic process, and to obey the law. In Socrates' case, ruthless criticism found its limit, its Tact and Taste, in his desire for the Law. This tension, between Desire for the Law and obedience to an inner calling, has been a constitutive part of the Western tradition ever since. The story of its vicissitudes is vast and complex.

During the European Middle Ages, argues Max Weber, Socrates' and other daemons were corralled and tamed by the life-enhancing embrace of a church that ruled in God's name. For millennia, the daemons were successfully banished into the night. They were permitted to show themselves among the living only under special circumstances: when purification rites became expected repetitions. In the long run, however, such cleansing acts were not enough. Beginning with the Renaissance, but particularly by the seventeenth century, as the sociopolitical structures of the Middle Ages gave way to the nascent capitalist system, the daemons began to gain in strength. By the middle of the nineteenth century, they had overcome their fetters and guards. Goethe reinstated the urgency of the Socratic tension in the nineteenth century. He wrote of the daemonic:

> It was not divine, for it seemed irrational; it was not human, for it had no reason; not devilish, for it was beneficent; not angelic, for it often allowed room for malice. It resembled the accidental, for it was without consequence; it looked like providence, for it hinted at hidden connections. Everything that restricts us seemed permeable by it; it seemed to arrange at will the necessary elements of our existence; it contracted time, it expanded space. It seemed at ease only in the impossible, and it thrust the possible from itself with contempt.[1]

QUESTIONABLE QUESTIONS

By asking anew very old questions, Nietzsche gave the socratic tension its clearest modern statement.[2] Who is the being bearing questionable questions? What lurks beneath the reasonable? What has been tamed, pushed under, bribed, but never ignored? That in the end Nietzsche embraced blind biology as the source and abode of all our daemons is beside the point. That having asked the same questions Freud thought he had found the adequate answers, based on biology first and in metaphysics later, is not the point. These were only two among many proffered solutions to the problem of having old daemons loosed on the world. Because with the easing of the embrace of the church—a church now fragmented and reduced to asking scientific reason for help to corral old and new daemons alike—new answers to very old questions were needed. Much of the hermeneutic effort over the last century has been geared to provide such new answers. Even by the time Max Weber came to think about the matter, however, in the context of a radicalized modernity where old and new daemons carried on trampling all sacred and profane places, it seemed the ancient ways of corralling and purifying no longer worked. Against his dearest wishes, therefore, Max Weber counseled us to embrace the daemons. Each one of us, he said, ought to embrace the daemon that holds the fibers of our very life and face the world armed only with what Lukacs would call "virile maturity"; with the utter conviction that there never was a God who made our choices; that Good and Evil pulsate from the center of our all-too-human hearts.

VARGAS LLOSA'S DAEMONS

It is to this already long tradition that Vargas Llosa attaches himself. Like Socrates, he tells us, he is driven by daemons; he does not choose his themes, they choose him.[3] Because of the long trajectory of Western culture, however, the ancient daemons reach us in a different light. In our postmodern world, we Good

Europeans—to borrow Nietzsche's felicitous phrase—do not have God to help us fend off their lure. In our world, Vargas Llosa accepts, there are only stunted gods competing with their ancient enemies. We might as well accept that, for better or for worse, these stunted gods and daemons are the only poles around which our lives can gather significance. This means we must accept, as Max Weber did but with a lighter heart, that these gods and daemons have made their home in the all-too-human, subjective world. We must accept, even embrace, radical subjectivity. This is, in part at least, what Lukacs had in mind when he asked us to exhibit "virile maturity." Postmodernist theorists—from Lacan to Foucault to Derrida—seem to have heeded the call.

There are critics for whom Vargas Llosa, particularly in view of his later works, must be considered as standing alongside the aforementioned postmodernist thinkers.[4] The relativized and fractionalized subjective and social world he offers in his fiction, plus his seemingly radical embrace of freedom in the political and cultural realm, make such positioning tempting. But such consideration would be at least partially incorrect. For here, too, Vargas Llosa oscillates. As will be clear as we proceed, deep down, Vargas Llosa is unwilling to embrace radical subjectivity, although he often appears to do so. In reality, his notion of the daemonic hovers somewhere between old Christian ideas regarding the efficacy of the soul and modern radical biology.[5] Perhaps more than anything, Vargas Llosa relies—as did many social theorists in the nineteenth century—on a personally nuanced and tacit understanding of core values of the Western tradition.

SUBJECTIVE AND SOCIAL DIMENSIONS

If we take radical subjectivity as the seat of our daemons, we can think of them as issuing from such feelings as resentment, anger, pride, and the like. They might also issue from the erotic dimension. In other words, if we follow Vargas Llosa, these daemons would appear to be of a "psychological" nature.[6] But the articulation of a psychological theory regarding such daemons in Vargas Llosa's oeuvre is far from complete. It is no accident, therefore, that sometimes he talks as if his daemons were spiritual beings mediating transcendent and temporal realms and draws closer to Goethe, and sometimes he writes as if they were organic in some sense. Such conceptual oscillation is not idiosyncratic. Psychological theories have always oscillated between spiritual and material explanations.

The conception of daemons as inhabiting our subjective world is complicated enough. But the matter gets even more complicated, as Vargas Llosa holds that daemons are not only individually grounded but can also be intersubjective, that is, historical and cultural in nature.[7] Insofar as we are sensual, social, and meaning-generating beings, Vargas Llosa holds, we must inhabit a social world whose demands we internalize. These demands turn into daemons working inside us as conscience or moral and intellectual expectations. Daemons embody sociological sediments.

Vargas Llosa does not wish to go so far as to argue for a social determinist view of the personality. Even when he was under Sartre's influence—as when he wrote his first major novel, *La ciudad y los perros,* for example, and portrayed human freedom as dramatically curtailed by childhood experiences and institutional constraints—he never took a decisive step toward radical social determinism. His valuation of individual freedom and choice was always strong enough to blunt the hard edge of fate—at least with regard to the Few who, through their art, can lift themselves out of the morass of the mundane. He does appreciate the insights of Western social theory, from Marx to Aron: the social sediment, the cultural heritage inside each one of us, exercises an important influence in the kinds of themes we choose and the types of daemons that rule us. This notion of Conscience and Desire follows from his belief that humans are not created beings; we are socially constructed, albeit in ways we do not yet fully understand. But such construction, he believes, necessitates rather than precludes the possibility of being freed from the constraints of the past.

FREEDOM AND THE DAEMONIC

At the level of subjectivity and at the level of the social world, then, the writer is not free to choose his daemons or his themes. On the one hand, he feels urges beyond his conscious control; on the other, the social world provides the field of action and the means with which to battle or to appease such urges. For Vargas Llosa the urges cannot be wished away; the armoire of tools at our disposal to deal with them cannot be wished into existence. Daemons are not, can never be, of our own individual making. Humans are, it seems, the occasion, the site for a battle waged between two obscure forces.

In this conception of the daemonic, Vargas Llosa oscillates to come full circle to the old saw concerning the duality of human nature: as a secular thinker he takes his lead from social and psychological theories from Marx to Freud; as a lapsed Catholic, he is unable to abandon his awe for and reliance on the miraculous.

DUALITY AND FREEDOM

Durkheim taught a whole generation of French intellectuals—among them some of Vargas Llosa's intellectual masters, such as Aron, Bataille, Camus, and Sartre—that the fateful duality of our nature is not something we ought to bemoan. On the contrary, and in a fundamental sense, it is precisely in the interstice between these two aspects of the human condition that freedom resides. The confrontation between individual desires and the cultural daemons embedded in morality and intellect serves as the occasion for the possibility of rebellion and creativity. Without individual urges, creativity would not be possible; without the social element the creative urge would have no form. Vargas Llosa, it seems, has made Durkheim's theoretical offerings his own.

THE CALLING

A writer, declares Vargas Llosa, ought to heed Max Weber's counsel and make his daemon the sole pole around which to organize his life. He must strike the posture of a virile maturity.

This means several things. First of all, it means that, in giving himself totally to his daemon, the writer risks opening himself up to the scrutiny and, perhaps, the incomprehension of the Many. This is because he must often exploit his deepest fears, his most cherished sentiments, his love of self and others, to express a Truth that transcends any particular attachment or obligation. He must be willing to exploit the feelings—love, hatred, pity, respect, envy—that others have toward him, for the sake of his overriding daemon. He must also be willing to use any and all material available to him in the social world (reports, confidential memos, overheard conversations, confessions, dictionaries, dreams) as raw materials for his aesthetic offerings. As the writer carries on, Vargas Llosa tells us, he must be prepared to suffer the ignominy of not being understood by the Many, on whose behalf he often offers his Truth; they might confuse his sacred obedience with the callous deeds of a manipulator.

If the writer is not responsible for the demands of his daemon, however, he is responsible for the form in which such demands coalesce and become accessible to the Many. According to Vargas Llosa, it is around such responsibility that the writer draws the circle of his ethics. The writer's responsibility is an aesthetic one. His personal idiosyncrasies, his character, must ultimately be judged against the literary accomplishments for which he uses his subjective and objective booty. The ethical justification for the writer's craft in the eyes of the Many is anchored on the idea that, in obeying his daemon, in achieving the adequate form, he enhances Freedom and Truth.

DISTINCTIONS

This understanding of the writer's calling engages the distinction between good or bad literature. If geniuses can claim to be free from the ethical standards of the Many because of their aesthetic achievements, how are we to distinguish between great and mediocre writers and separate both from those who might claim to be but are not accomplished artists at all? How do we ground ethics on aesthetics? In the Western past, the likes of Kant and Schiller could draw fast distinctions on these matters mainly because they still adhered to what they believed was a universal conception of Beauty. In their world, Taste and Tact, as boundaries for the aesthetically permissible, were still communal categories.[8] Without such a conception, in a relativist world where only stunted gods and daemons roam, how do we ground the aesthetic judgment?

In our postmodern world, the daemons of which Vargas Llosa speaks do not possess tacitly accepted preemptive claims. In the first place, why should we, the Many, even believe that such urges exist, since they apparently do not "hold the fibers of our very lives"? And even if we agree as to their existence, why should we tolerate them? In a relativist world, which Vargas Llosa often urges us to embrace, daemons cannot borrow strength from the cultural residues used to ground ultimate values or Truth. In such a world, aesthetics can no longer ground universal ethical claims and a writer's offerings are only one more product in the capitalist inventory of values and ideas.

LATIN AMERICAN DAEMONS

Vargas Llosa developed his art in clear opposition to the Latin American tradition of fiction writing, which he has always considered quite amateurish. In large part, he has noted, this was because most authors writing before the midcentury saw their art as a means to something else. This was particularly so among those who saw literature as a political tool, as was the case with the Indigenista writers. In those cases, the correct message was more important than the form. Such writers saw themselves as cultural leaders in the broadest sense and hence their dedication to their art, their embrace of their daemons, was suspect.[9] Very few let the aesthetic daemons rule their hearts.

Reviewing his long struggle to free himself from the weight of what he considers a dismal past, we can say that perhaps Vargas Llosa has been only partially successful. Quite undeniably, his literature and his politics have always been deeply connected; precisely where the form of his fiction itself is concerned.[10] And he has been altogether unable to escape the role of cultural leader, in the broader sense of the term.

ASCETIC AESTHETICS

Like most other bourgeois writers, Vargas Llosa has always wished to be able to live off and for literature. That is, he has always wished to be successful in the marketplace; to be a professional writer. When he was a marxist, the ground for this stance was, contra Marx's epigoni, generally aesthetic. The dedication to his art, as we have seen, approached the acceptance of a calling: art could say something meaningful about the issues of the day. Later on, when he became a neoliberal and his conception of the Market as the adequate adjudicatory agency for the worth of human activity grew, his conception of the professional writer tilted toward considerations of material success. It had to, since in the neoliberal ideology, money is the only medium of exchange for goods and services, aesthetic or otherwise.

What has remained constant throughout these changes, however, has been Vargas Llosa's belief that the writer's art requires a serious, methodical approach. This is in two senses: first, the aesthetic dimension has a decisive intentional, rational component. This is what Vargas Llosa admired in Flaubert's feverish approach to writing.[11] In the feverish yet intention-full mood, the writer exploits subjective and objective worlds for the sake of his daemon. Second, the aesthetic dimension requires a methodical life as well. The Hemingwayian bouts of inspiration are siren calls for Vargas Llosa. The only guarantee of aesthetic accomplishment is hard work. Max Weber might have been right: the ascetic animus, which began as an active shunning of the aesthetic, is now quite at home in the realm of pleasure. By this criterion, Vargas Llosa judges that most Latin American writers are not serious about their art.

CHAOS AND FORM

Given this feverish yet intention-full mood, the process of form giving is, in principle, infinite. The subjective and the social worlds are fully at the disposal of art and neither can provide, on its own, the necessary asymptotes or parameters for the adequate aesthetic form. In addition, to be true to his daemon the writer must be open to hearing the cacophony of voices from the subjective and objective worlds. Such a cacophony of voices is, needless to say, never ending and chaotic. If the psychological and social magma is to coalesce into an aesthetic form, the writer's rational, intention-full approach must intervene. Reason enters as the stern molder in the creative act. For the writer must decide which voices to silence and which to privilege. It is in this context that Vargas Llosa's intention to produce a Total Novel must be understood.

THE TOTAL NOVEL

In Vargas Llosa's conception, the Total Novel translates an attempt to bring essential aspects of the chaotic subjective and social world into adequate form. It is an attempt to express the total reality, including its facticity and its felt absences. This animus makes the novel a preeminent critical art.[12] And yet, the Total Novel is not an infinite novel. It is an achieved form, which, at its best, retains the seen and unseen Truths of the times.

Until recently, Vargas Llosa held that to let these Truths issue forth unencumbered, the author must strive to become invisible. Impartiality is the contemporary writer's master virtue.[13] In today's world, too visible an author can only produce what Lukacs in his Hegelian moment called a "bad infinity."

GLIMPSES

In a wonderful essay, "The Task of the Translator," Walter Benjamin notes that there are truths that are ineffable through any given language but can be glimpsed through the intention implicit in all languages. The art of translation aims at highlighting such glimpses. As for a language capable of conveying such glimpsed Truths, a pure language, it is unattainable as far as humans are concerned.

We could approach Vargas Llosa's notion of the Total Novel in a similar vein. In his view, each succeeding piece of writing forms part of the indispensable magma for future literature. Within a given tradition, through their accumulating particular truths, writers offer glimpses of a larger Truth. For this reason, the writer of the Total Novel strives to replace God. He does not only aim to grasp that which is, but also that which has been, might be, or ought to be. The past, as history and biography, are essential components of this totalizing vision.[14] So are the visions of alternative ways of being. In short, the Total Novel offers the felicitous occasion for the rich presentation of *elementos añadidos*.

PROMETHEAN TENDENCIES

In his philosophical inquiry into the novel form, Georg Lukacs believed he had found that only irony could save it from either turning into mere entertainment or closing the circle too soon by showing the European world as an integrated totality. Irony kept the tension between the real and the possible and hence allowed for a positive critique. Eventually, of course, Lukacs came to believe, as had Marx, that communism would usher in an integrated civilization that reconnected humanity with the happier ages of the past. To Vargas Llosa, Lukacs's is an already old vision; a vision flushed away, together with the promises it embodied, in a derailed socialist revolution. We postmodernists ought to know, he claims, that there never was, nor could there ever be, an integrated civilization. We ought to know that the most we can ever hope for is a healthy, though temporary, equilibrium of market forces.

If this is so, irony can no longer play the role assigned to it by Lukacs in the aesthetic of the novel. Rather, it can only be just one more element in the writer's inventory of tools used for a realistic portrayal of our world. As with Tact and Taste—guiding communal categories so deftly analyzed first by Lukacs and then by Gadamer—irony can no longer function as a corroding element to a self-certain posture. For Vargas Llosa, there cannot be self-certain postures in the postmodern world. The only certainty allowed (ironically) is that nothing is certain. In particular, self-certain idealist postures, argues Vargas Llosa, are disguised ideologies with totalitarian intentions; they are a thing of the past. In truth, utopia is not something we ought to pursue; what is realizable of its promise is already at hand in the capitalist formations that rule our world. Hence, irony is no longer woven into the form of the novel; it coalesces in a character—often a writer— and it is thus accounted for as one more element of the deicidal act.

TACT AND TASTE

When he wrote *The Theory of the Novel*, Lukacs still felt the influence of Kant's mischievous notion of genius, although the Hegelian move from *Moralität* to *Sittlichkeit* had already been decisive. Still, in his account of the creative act, Tact and Taste are seen as indispensable categories; they are the limits imposed by the community against the Promethean tendencies of the individual. It was because he could not ignore these communal categories, argued Gadamer later on, that an author was able to dispense wisdom.

To Vargas Llosa, such notions are obsolete. Tact and Taste, like the ironic, more properly belong to characters in the fictive world of the Total Novel. In our times, the aesthetic daemon has finally gained freedom from communal accountability. The contemporary Promethean writer, unlike the genius of old, proclaims his freedom from the moral hold of the Many: "it seemed to arrange at will the necessary elements of our existence."

3

+

On Truthtelling

All this means: basically and from time immemorial we are—accustomed to lying. Or to put it more virtuously and hypocritically, in short, more pleasantly: one is much more of an artist than one knows.

—F. Nietzsche

CONCEPTS

By the end of the nineteenth century, Western intellectuals had firmly established the claim that concepts, the building blocks of thought, were not given to us by God, since He himself is only a concept. Rather, concepts have been fashioned upon biological ground over the long trajectory of human development. To the moderns, History made sense: after a long travail, humans could finally understand their sometimes blind but always upward movement toward ever greater Consciousness and Freedom.

Over the last fifty years, but following Nietzsche, postmodern intellectuals have argued fiercely that all concepts—that of History included—bear the all-too-human marks of power and resentment. These marks explain why, at least since Plato, we have built on the error that concepts have a power all their own. From Plato's Intelligible World to Hegel's overly serious claim that phenomena strive to achieve their Notion, such theories have obeyed ulterior motives. They have often translated the interest of caste and class; they have often been pure mystical chatter. As Marx himself pointed out, History wages no battles. Power and Desire, postmodern intellectuals argue, are the real forces in all thinking and valuing.

GOOD EUROPEANS

The radical iconoclastic insight was developed by the moderns, despite their often veiled respect for theological residues. For the moment when, over against miracle and faith, Reason proclaimed its self-sufficiency and ventured to explain life and the cosmos, it began the inevitable collapse of all Intelligible Worlds. But the true dimensions of this insight—the undermining of any and all ultimate positions—have only been fully played out in our lifetimes. For now, even Reason, which had first disclosed the marks of Power and Desire in all thinking and valuing, is suspect; it, too, is seen as bearing the marks of the all-too-human. As a consequence, few among us postmoderns dare abide by such distinctions as between *Vernunft* and *Verstand*, Reason and understanding. Even fewer can still shiver in awe (publicly, at least) before the shrinking realm of the sacred, apparently the last and only refuge for universal concepts. Most postmodern intellectuals would rather follow Nietzsche in his Dionysian dance and display "virile maturity."

But how did these postmodern Good Europeans[1]—virile philosophers of radical suspicion—come to exhibit such daring and courage? This is an important question; it lies at the core of contemporary self- and cultural understanding. Now that God is apparently dead and only daemons roam the world; now that we have apparently undermined all ultimate values: how exactly do we show "virile maturity" and embrace the relativism and even nihilism that remain? Are we postmoderns, fastidious heirs to the Enlightenment, really willing and able to abandon all crutches? Or do we follow Nietzsche to the end, and sneak in an essentialist sin? It seems the latter. For despite all our relativist posturing, we postmodern intellectuals seem to cuddle a universalizing desire: in truth, only our Truths are really true.

GLOBALIZATION

The disavowed, and hence powerful, desire only increases with the processes of globalization, a postmodern phenomenon par excellence. Because, at its core, the postmodern stance necessitates the acknowledgment of a multicultural world; the theory is designed to give each alternative culture due consideration, before dismissing it as clearly misguided or plainly primitive.[2] These cultures are dismissable precisely because they exhibit foundational values, and, plainly, no truly civilized society could possibly tolerate being under the sway of universal concepts. Thus, the postmodern stance assumes a privileged position as it rides the "civilizing" forces of the West. The claim that only relative truths are really true cannot obey national boundaries. The transvaluation of ultimate values must become a cosmic affair. The harangue has echoed around the world. In fact, the often highly articulated justification of relativism is now even found—or, should we say, precisely found—at the periphery of the Western, Nietzschean world.

WOULD-BE GOOD EUROPEANS

Stubbornly, the non-Western world continues to embrace Ultimate Truths. Universal concepts still cement a way of life quite foreign to the Good Europeans. These Truths have made non-Western cultures recalcitrant to seeing life and the cosmos in Western terms—that is, as fully civilized human beings. This was one of the main reasons, we ought to recall, why Karl Marx hoped capitalism would do away with such Truths altogether.

Over the last five centuries, the destruction of non-Western cultures has been accomplished under the animus of the more powerful Western Ultimate Truths. Christianity first and Science later—both in concert with the Market—dispersed to replace older asymptotes for living and dying at the periphery of the West. And all through these centuries, there have been intellectuals among the conquered who, more than anything, have desired to be Western, to belong to the tradition of Plato, Aquinas, Kant, Hegel, Marx, and Freud. In short, the destruction of non-Western Ultimate Truths and their unremitting replacement by the values of Western Modernity—which, then as now, claimed universality—has been done by collusion.[3]

COLONIALS

In Latin America, the imposed modern asymptotes have been in place for half a millennium. But now, reflecting, yet again, the cultural effervescence of Europe, the process of replacing modern Truths is afoot in the former colonies. Christian, marxist, even scientistic asymptotes are under attack by inspired native intellectuals. There is talk about the postmodern condition in boulevards and coffeehouses; there is a search for new values for changed circumstances. The postmodern desire to end all ideology—and hence tradition—by seeing everything as ideological has reached impressive heights. Many believe the continent is living through fateful times. Buoyed by the borrowed material and cultural forces of postmodernity, some believe Latin Americans could finally embrace—and perhaps what is more important, be embraced by—Europe; they could finally shed all the residues of barbarism and belong in the universal culture.[4] Enlightenment, via electronic links or access to markets, appears finally at hand. The question is how to better utilize the opportunities offered by a postmodern world where everything is possible, from reconstructing gender to renegotiating national identities.

TRUTHTELLING

Modern social theorists—heirs to the Enlightenment—claimed to have shown that a lie is a lie only if it passes for a truth. Where there is no possibility for truth, there is no possibility for lies. The reverse holds: without the possibility of lies there is no truth. This is so because concepts are contextual. In a situation where everyone tells the same lie, it ceases to be. In a situation where no one lies, there is no truth. Truth and untruth are twin human constructs. But modern social theorists such as Marx, Weber, Freud, and Durkheim never really abandoned the notion that some Truths are better, or higher, than others. The Truths of Science and Reason, in particular, were taken as superior to those issuing from aesthetic inspiration or mystical revelation.

Until recently, outrage against a lie was the privilege of those who held fast to some Truths. Such Truths were never the property of individuals, of course. Soothsayers, Lawgivers, or saints all spoke the language of their communities. Their ultimate valuations were grounded on faith, memory, or hope. But even as recent an offering as Kant's conception of genius was never self-indulgent. The genius's task and privilege was to show the rest of mortals glimpses of the noumenal world and thus feed their hope of an eventual union with the Divine, in the Kingdom of Ends.

Such views of Truth are quite naive and parochial, for the Good and Would-Be Good Europeans. Postmodern intellectuals know that many such Truths have hobbled along, often clashing irreconcilably, over the vast expanses of space and time. After millennia they have been diminished by their mutual animosity, and now not one of them has the power to tempt and overwhelm us any more. Perhaps. For it is true that Marx's wishes and predictions are coming true: around the world, all truths are being dissolved in the icy waters of calculation. What Marx saw as a temporary condition, as a stage in the inevitable march of humanity through time, now threatens to become permanent. Perhaps due to disillusion or fatigue, around the world people seem on the brink of embracing one Truth: the Market.

POSTMODERNS AND NEOLIBERALS

The two new currents of thought among Western intellectuals, postmodernism and neoconservativism, seem to concur in seeing the Market as the best ground for Truth in our times. Postmodern intellectuals claim to have grasped the power-smeared Truth behind the ebb and flow of contemporary life: everything is constructed and hence potentially negotiable. Each postmodern individual is a producer and a consumer of identities, images, dreams, and desires. Authenticity, like the Individual, is a thing of the past. For their part, horrified neoliberals take a step backward: the apparently chaotic and negotiable ebb and flow of life is, in Truth, determined by our Human Nature, God-given for some, historically attained for others.[5] In both cases, there is a tightness of fit between human potentialities and the Market as adjudicator of all possibilities.

It is in this context—in the nexus of old (Protestant and modern) and new (post-modern) valuations—that the sociopolitical theories of Vargas Llosa must be understood. For, as in other matters, he manages to straddle both currents of thought.

PERUVIAN TRUTHTELLERS

Writer/critic Augusto Salazar Bondy (1927–74), one of the clearest thinkers of his generation, was furious with the upper classes of Peru for not calling things by their true name, for practicing self-deception.[6] As he looked around, he found the self-appointed intellectual representatives of that class suffering from a serious dis-ease: neocolonialism. Having absorbed his lucid critique, to be fair, we can say that such dis-ease is not unique to Peru. It has been detected all over the world.[7] Entire continents seem to have succumbed before its power. But in Peru, in Lima, to be exact, Salazar Bondy noted that the dis-ease had issued in a perverse distinction: that between *vivos* ("savvy") and *tontos* (naive). Unlike the *vivos*, the *tontos* are unable to lie, cheat, simulate, or dissimulate for the sake of personal advantages.[8]

Salazar Bondy has not been alone in carrying out a cleansing criticism of the upper classes of Peru. On the contrary, he exemplifies a long tradition of Peruvian intellectuals who have periodically risen to unmask lies. Just before him, for example, the iconoclast Manuel Gonzales Prada claimed to have detected the pus of Truth under the scab of the *vivos*'s lies. Soon after, Gonzales Prada's famous disciple, José Carlos Mariátegui, indicted the Peruvian upper classes' greed, armed with Marx's insights into the mechanisms of oppression. Even César Vallejo, that poet of plain suffering, used words and deeds to tell his lacerating Truth. More recently, Gustavo Gutierrez, the founder of Liberation Theology, has re-proclaimed the Truth of the Father, Son, and Holy Ghost, against contemporary misappropriations and deceptions. Indeed, Peruvians seem to have been Truthtellers for quite some time. What is important to note in all these Truthtelling efforts is that the *vivos*'s deceptions have always been seen against a background of essential Truths.

TONTOS

Postmodern Peruvian intellectuals are suspicious of these and any other Truth-full positions. They find such Truthtellers childish; tyros in a world finally devoid of easy illusions. The old freethinkers and iconoclasts simply believed too much; they were easily seduced by grammar and other all-too-human facts. Some of them were still caught in the webs of religious deception; others were imprisoned by totalitarian thinking. They were all *tontos* after all.

POSTMODERN TRUTHTELLER

On this issue Mario Vargas Llosa, the most celebrated Peruvian writer/critic of our time—and a most interesting Truthteller in his own right—appears to side with the postmodern intellectuals. But, in reality, he straddles both camps. On the one hand, he has risen against the mass of Peruvian Truthtellers to ask them to abandon their naive embrace of Truth. He demands that they trade it in for a frank acceptance that all concepts, Truth and its opposite included, are all-too-human constructs. On the other, he holds these views with absolute conviction.

Vargas Llosa claims that his bold call for a change of heart does not issue from a selfish or narrow standpoint. Rather, it comes out of his love for humanity. For, in addition to our naive love of Truths, we humans have a desperate, though often denied, need for Lies.[9] Only Lies, he argues, can save us from the oppressive power of certainty. Given his overall sociopolitical views, he posits that among such Lies, self-imposed ones are best. And since he is an accomplished practitioner, it is not surprising to know that for him the clearest exemplars of such needed Lies are to be found in literature. By immersing ourselves in fictive worlds, he claims, we humans aim to satisfy our need to lie to ourselves.

It turns out, then, that past writers and critics, convinced Truthtellers all, were not truthful enough. They did not call literature and all ideological constructions by their real name: seductive Lies. They fooled themselves and their readers by calling their fiction and theories confessions, articulated hopes, truthful descriptions, or projective dreams of worlds to come. As a Peruvian, heir to a long tradition of Truthtellers, Vargas Llosa wishes to call *al pan pan y al vino vino*: literature and all ideologies are nothing more nor less than Lies we tell ourselves. In the case of literature: the better the Lie, the better the literature, and vice versa.

LIES AND LIFE

Vargas Llosa wishes to say something more. He wishes to proclaim that Lies are essential for life itself. Exemplifying virile maturity, he dares to embrace the world as it is, not as we wish it to be. And the naked truth is that all humans are liars. More still: that if we are not liars, we ought to be. Because, without useful Lies, we would end up killing each other.[10] Lies are essential for human survival.

THE GOOD LIE

To write literature is to lie, according to Vargas Llosa. To write good literature is to lie well. And, as we have seen, to write well the writer must engage his or her craft with determination, premeditation, and rationality. In other words, the application of method to object, a central legacy of the Enlightenment's search for Truth, in this case obeys the desire to fashion a Good Lie. However, since Vargas Llosa shares the postmodern view that Lying is the twin companion of Truthtelling, that Truth and its opposite are mutually defined constructions that emerge, hobbling, not like Minerva, out of our mundane existence, he holds that, not only the Will to Lie, but also the Will to Truth abides at the heart of literature. Through its subtle arsenal of lies, he posits, literature lets out its Truth, even if only tangentially, shyly, masked.[11]

What, then, is the fundamental Truth brought forth by the Good Lie? That the world is more complex than it first appears; that there are no Ultimate Truths; that Good and Evil are twin forces inhabiting the human heart; that there is more to life than death; that there is more to death than just rewards. Of course, Vargas Llosa notes, because of resilient residues of outmoded valuations, because of childishness, even today, the Many abhor such Truths and are still determined to banish them into the night. Only in fiction do such Truths find a safe haven. And even there, they are often covered over, sidestepped, by the self-deception of author and readers.[12] Only now, perhaps, as the postmodern world and its intellectual vanguard rise to the occasion, are we nearly ready to accept these Truths.

There is more. Truthtelling today, Vargas Llosa notes, exacts a high price. The writers of fiction—those noble miracle workers, daring keepers of the gateway for Truth—are wont to be called names, to be castigated as amoral, and overall suffer the darts and arrows of incomprehension. But they cannot help themselves. For they are possessed. Their daemons urge them to speak their Truth. In the end, therefore, these Good European equivalents must embrace their calling and stand, alone and misunderstood, beyond Good and Evil. They must hold dear to their literature as the Many hold on to their dreams; they must claim the right to dream freely; they must defend literature, the last sacrosanct residence of Freedom, from the assault of misguided dolts and their regimes of Truths.[13] For it is not as private dreaming that literature exhibits its noblest Truth. On the contrary, to let its Truth shine forth, literature must confront the mesmerizing, concealing, moral world of the ignorant Many and their masters.

IN THE BEGINNING . . .

The characters in Vargas Llosa's fiction inhabit chaotic worlds where Truth and untruth, dream and reality, fantasy and existence commingle. In such worlds, one might suspect, the possibilities for freedom could be abundant. But such is not the case. To the contrary, Vargas Llosa's characters always seem at the mercy of intractable external and internal forces. Under such circumstances, Freedom is understood as "freedom from" such constraints. We do often find characters struggling against the odds. But their attempts to free themselves nearly always end in utter failure. At most, some particularly insightful characters learn to face the world free from illusions; they develop virile maturity and accept that the world is ruled by power, corruption, and lies. But then, as a consequence of their insight, they end up simulating and dissimulating like everyone else.

In Vargas Llosa's fictive worlds, lies are common bonds and common bonds are lies. Religions, we are often reminded, are not only mass delusions; they are also the artwork of creative minds who stir the cinders of collective desires.[14] Echoing Freud's daring revision of Genesis, Vargas Llosa believes that, in the beginning, there was Fiction. Fiction is the foundational deed of civilization. Freud must be taken at his word: the killing of the Father was only a "just so" story. The mark of humanity's maturity is the ability to see the Foundational Fiction for what it really is. Once that is attained, Fiction can be safely placed where it belongs: in litera-ture. From there, free from its constraints, Fiction can continue to offer its merely imaginary, but absolutely necessary, visions of salvation. As Freud thought of crime and dreaming, Vargas Llosa thinks of lying and literature: it would be bet-ter if we were to satisfy our need for lies by writing and reading fiction.

THE GOLDEN LIE

In not-quite-mature areas of the world—in Latin America, for example—lying has not yet been tamed and safely deposited in its proper place. Rather, lying suf-fuses everything; it multiplies everywhere. For Vargas Llosa, such cultures seem caught in a veritable limbo: the Fictional Foundations no longer work, and rational habits and valuations have not yet acquired weight and solidity. Post-modernity has caught them unprepared. This is one reason why the fictive Peru-vian reality is shown as inhabited by individuals constantly lying, in order to sur-vive in a manicheistic world where Good and Evil are felt in their all-too-human dimensions.[15] These characters, *vivos* all, are willing to betray themselves and those closest to them for the sake of survival. Adorno and Horkheimer's deepest fears, that Ego overturn Superego and embrace mimesis for the sake of survival, it seems, have come true on the periphery of the West.[16]

In Peru, Vargas Llosa offers in his Truth-full fiction that the aim of all partic-ular lies is to keep what José Miguel Oviedo has called the "Golden Lie" hidden from view. That is, little lies sustain the big lie that there indeed are essential rules governing our mundane existence. Nothing could be further from the Truth, according to Vargas Llosa's fiction. There are no rules, save those tainted by power and resentment and hence inherently capricious. This is why we do not find good institutions in Vargas Llosa's fictive world, despite sporadic good intentions on the part of individuals living under their tutelage. The army, the courts, the church, the family, the political parties all exact simulation and dis-simulation. In such a world, the words of Cayo Bermudez become effective pass-words: "Don't trust even your mother."[17] The Peru of Vargas Llosa's fictive world is so terrible, so shot through with power and resentment, that even Nature is deceptive, precisely when it appears to calm and to nurture us.[18]

A MODERN TRUTHTELLER

It would appear from the foregoing that there never are nor could be heroes in Vargas Llosa's fictive world. But such a reading of his lifework would be at least partially incorrect. Given Vargas Llosa's conception of himself and his art, it is not surprising that the unlikely hero in many of his works turns out to be the writers of fictions. These characters escape the weight of their milieux and the sediment of internal traumas, in and through their imagination. In a position resembling Kant's conception of freedom—as something internal to the individual—and against Hannah Arendt's conception of freedom as something won or lost at the level of the social, Vargas Llosa's characters are really free only as they give wings to their imagination, particularly in the creation of fictive worlds. In other words, individuals are "free to" act in the world, to give form to their dreams and their hopes, only by turning their backs on the world around them. Contrary to the utopic animus exemplified by movements from early Christianity to Marxism, Vargas Llosa's fiction, which is consonant with his current sociopolitical views, proffers the notion that the only world humans can make comply with the demands of their thoughts and their desires is the one they can invent.[19]

GLAUCON'S CHALLENGE

In Plato's Republic, the agreeable Glaucon poses an interesting question to Socrates; a question about Justice. He recounts a story about one of Gyges' ancestors who had found a gold ring with the power of making its wearer invisible. The lucky man could live as he pleased, immunized by his invisibility. With such a ring, Glaucon asks, why should any man be just and obey the Law? Glaucon's question remained relevant in Western philosophy for millennia. It retained the full force of its power all through the European Enlightenment. In fact, modern social theory could be understood as an effort to answer the problem with the help of Reason alone. In our postmodern world, however, Glaucon's question does not command the same attention. Indeed, if the Law (like all other fundamental rules for social life) is a construction grounded in lies we share, why should we obey it if we can transgress it with impunity? Ought we not to see all such constructions as pragmatic rules at the service of our individual desires?

AMBIVALENCES

On this issue, too, Vargas Llosa's position is ambivalent. On the one hand, he wishes to retain a moral dimension to his work—including, of course, Truthtelling; on the other, he embraces a utilitarian approach to morality—including deception and simulation. As was noted before, he is more than willing to circumvent the Law of the Many for the sake of the Good Lie urged by his daemon. He justifies the transgression by appealing to a higher, more sublime obligation. But what of Vargas Llosa not as author but as ordinary citizen?

LYING IN LIFE

He is not shy in admitting having deceived for the sake of personal advantages. He tells us, for example, that protected by his privileged position in a neocolonial society—the equivalent of the gold ring—he passed for an agrarian expert, university leader, revolutionary, and politico. What could be his justification for having failed to live up to Camus's strictures never to commit or justify, under any circumstances, lying and crime?[20] The Sartrean answer to the question is quite straightforward: it is the fact of having been born in a country of dullards where ignorance and unbridled passion is fertile soil for fiction and lies.[21]

In his autobiographical writing Vargas Llosa tells us that such a cruel world undermined his innocence very early on. His parents' marriage broke up under the pressures of class prejudices and half-truths. A protective myth was then woven by the Llosa clan to fend off the danger his father represented; a danger that turned out to be real enough. Within the Llosa clan his uncle Lucho showed him how to deceive.[22] Later Vargas Llosa was sexually abused by a priest. Later still, as a youth in search of identity, he was confronted by the dictatorship of Manuel A. Odria, which, he would write bitterly, produced a generation of Peruvians with "no heroes nor martyrs, only failures."[23] By the time he was old enough to marry his aunt-by-marriage, he had learned well to use the privileges of his class to his advantage.[24] Indeed, it appears, Vargas Llosa was taught to be a Peruvian *vivo* after all. He acquired a utilitarian approach to the Law through the ordeal of surviving in a hostile world.

Lying is so palpable in the doltish politics of Peru, he tells us, that it inevitably fosters inauthenticity and empty rhetoric.[25] And he confesses not to have developed a taste for the necessary accoutrements of Peruvian politics: a flair for the dramatic, pressing of the flesh, acceptance of "showers of the multitude."[26] And yet, for the sake of "the people," he ran for president in 1990. His interest was reluctant and amateurish at first. But Politics, that powerful modern daemon, demanded that he give up the Will to Truth and embrace the Will to Power. Drawing from past experiences, perhaps grudgingly, he simulated for his audiences a head of state before Lee Teng-hui and Toshiki Kaifu.[27] He tolerated dirty tricks, provocations, even deceptive subliminal messages in his campaign. For the sake of power, it seems, he played the game. The irony that the government of the righteous—a veritable postmodern antidote to totalitarianism and nurturant of multiple truths—was to issue from the application of tried methods of corrupt politics was lost from view.

WRITING, LYING, LIVING

To produce the Good Lie, Vargas Llosa tells us, a god-slayer author must become a vulture, ruthlessly feeding on all experiences. He must see everything in the world as possible material for his art. At the same time, he cannot prevent the necessary habit from tainting all of his human relations.[28] Gabriel García Márquez's attitude toward life, he notes, is a veritable example of an author's posture before the world. The man, he says, cannot help but see the world through the prism of his aesthetic sensitivity; he cannot help but become godlike, spin tall tales about his daily life, and transform his world as in a book.[29] Indeed, how to confine the Will to Lie within the borders of a book? And why?

UCHURACCAY

The commingling of fiction and reality outside the borders of a literary text is plain in Vargas Llosa's report on the tragedy of Uchuraccay. When he accepted President Fernando Belaunde Terry's call to head a fact-finding commission on the tragedy that had cost several journalists their lives, he construed the task as an occasion to defend Truth. Against the expectations of many, he attempted an "objective" report. But, despite his noble effort, it is quite difficult to distinguish the Will to Truth from the Will to Lie in that report. Sections of it read like portions of a novel: an ignorant, feverish, scared, violent, ferocious mass of primitive Indians attacked the innocent journalists. The imputation of a state of mind to the poor peasants, months after the event, without even the most rudimentary proof of such psychological assumptions, can only be conceived as an invention. Whether despite such shortcomings it still discloses a deeper Truth is something that can be debated.[30]

THE GREAT ESCAPE

The great European social theorists of the late nineteenth and early twentieth centuries rose determined to unmask Lies and to tell the Truth. Marx told of the destruction of all sacred values by the inexorable dialectic of History. Weber limited the explanatory power of nomothetic laws in human affairs. Durkheim showed the face of the all-too-human behind the sacred. Freud educated us for radical suspicion. Nietzsche questioned everything—except biology itself. In short, they were modern Lawgivers, ready to descend to our cave and show us the way to Truth.[31] But such figures, postmodern intellectuals argue, belong to an already old world. There in fact is no way out of our cave; and there is no Truth. Virile maturity means having to abandon such dreamy constructions.

There surely must be postmodern intellectuals who hold fast to their convictions, despite the gaping nihilism postmodernism fosters. But, as far as Vargas

Llosa is concerned, is he really willing to live without such grounding values? It does not appear so. After all, much like the modern Lawgivers, he envisions History moving unidirectionally—with the West moving ahead of the pack, of course—and holds fast to core values of Western culture, such as Truthtelling, Freedom, and Happiness. But even more significantly, and this time counter to his modern predecessors, he adds to the traditional array of Ultimate Values and boldly embraces the Market as the very foundation of modern civilization. In his fiction and other writings, he is helped by these Truths to steer clear of nihilism. He truly believes that the values and Truths that he holds are, in some essential way, worthier than those of others. His periodical jeremiads against his fellow Peruvians draw their moral strength from such utterly serious convictions.

4

✢

A Writer's Morality

Specialists without spirit, sensualists without heart; this nullity imagines that it has attained a level of civilization never before achieved.

—M. Weber

THE ANTINOMIES

The overcoming of the antinomies of Individual versus Society and Duty versus Desire, Vargas Llosa understands, comes with a high but necessary price. He also understands that, as Freud had articulated most clearly, this overcoming takes place at the expense of the individual. Society, Vargas Llosa accepts, needs to regulate and, if need be, repress the individual's freedom—expressed largely as deeply felt urges—for the sake of order, cohesiveness, and life itself. Furthermore, like Durkheim—who with Freud must be counted among the great secular moralists of our times—Vargas Llosa calls this regulation moral. In other words, he believes naked power could never succeed in exacting that high a price.

But Vargas Llosa departs from the Durkheimian position swiftly. To Durkheim, moral regulation is the sine qua non of our humanity itself; while Vargas Llosa furthers the Enlightenment's standpoint, exemplified by Freud's position: such moral regulation is mostly, if not solely, needed for the well-being of the Many.[1] Of course, this long-accepted split between the Few and the Many is problematic. Minimally, if we are to hold that morality is differently grounded depending on whether it involves the Enlightened Few or the Ignorant Many, then it behooves us to articulate such differing grounds. The easy dichotomy, drawn in the tradition of the nineteenth century and hence based on unexamined moral and developmental premises, is insufficient, at least now, as our millennium draws to a close.

REASONABLE SELF-INTEREST

There are at least three aspects in Vargas Llosa's moral theory that warrant discussion. The *first* and clearest aspect has to do with having Reason as the preferred and preeminent ground. In this case Vargas Llosa follows closely the moral theories of Durkheim and Freud: it is highly desirable that Ego stand firm where Id has been. The unidirectional movement of History guarantees that all of humanity will eventually achieve "virile maturity" and replace illusions and delusions with a realistic appraisal of our position in the cosmos. For, in the final analysis, humans are solely responsible for the strengths or weaknesses of the moral fabric that makes their lives possible. For now, of course, the Many are not yet capable of seeing this fundamental truth. Consequently, their morality is still preeminently guided by mystical tendencies and crude utility concerns.

This brings up the *second* aspect in Vargas Llosa's moral theory. He appears to be at once siding with and abandoning the position of modern social theorists. On the one hand, he sides with them by positing Reason as the ultimate ground for modern life. On the other, he holds that self-interest coincides or is consonant with a rational attitude toward the moral life. In other words, he seems to go against the views of social theorists who, from Kant to Freud, have always understood utilitarianism as an inadequate and even misguided ground for morality.

In this case, the ambivalence is only apparent. When it comes to morality—and this has become particularly clear more recently as he has embraced a fully neoliberal position—Vargas Llosa simply adheres to a different, narrower conception of Reason. In effect, he equates Reason with instrumental reason. In other words, the only type of social action for a rational individual in postmodernity is what Weber called *zweckrational* action: rational with respect to choice of means and ends, calculating on both counts, and mindful of the results. In this sense, Vargas Llosa's moral theory approaches a consequentialist ethics. Since all postmodern individuals are free agents in an ever more enlightened world made possible by capitalist economic and political formations, the worth of their moral choices can be judged with reference to their success or failure in the Market.

THE MARKET AND MORALITY

There is an interesting historical regression in Vargas Llosa's position: as in the heroic days of capitalism, when Puritan self-reliance and self-righteousness defied the established order, he believes the Few and the Many are differentiated—*sine ira et studio*—in terms of their success or failure in the Market. In effect, his is an updated version of Calvinism's Signification Corollary. In consonance with such views, Vargas Llosa believes that, as in the days when salvation, not only profit, was the motivation, personal worthiness can be glimpsed only if success is achieved through morally correct, rule-bound action. Unlike what Weber called adventure capitalism, modern capitalism requires that the successful Few exhibit sobriety and probity in their business activities. Such uprightness is self-interested: it is the only way for the chaos of the Market to be perceived as lawful and fair and to make sure the Many embrace and live up to the norms in place.

But the regression is not total. After all, Vargas Llosa claims that all religions, even the Protestant, are mass delusions. He wishes to ground morality in something other than blind faith. His views on the daily motivation for carrying on, selling and buying oneself, must, therefore, find other means of support. He finds this in the marriage between reason and egoism and the mechanical-seeming impartiality of the free market. He points to success stories to cement the notion that everyone is indeed, in principle, free to succeed or to fail. Failure is attributable to failings of the individual's reasoning or motivation; success is attributable to rule-bound constancy of effort. The exemplification of such freedom is reflected in modern Peruvian entrepreneurs—those who supported his candidacy—and by the so-called *informales* populating the urban centers in Peru.

In order to hold this view of the Market, Vargas Llosa must dismiss the long, thorough critique of that institution as the proper adjudicator of human worth: a critique carried out equally from the left and the right, from secular and religious thinkers, from Marx to Durkheim. At the same time, and crucially, he must radically minimize or ignore the fact that the required desire to embrace the rules of the game has always been based on grounds other than self-interest or utility concerns. For, today as in the past, the embrace of the Market as the adjudicatory force is ultimately grounded on an embrace of the nonsecular. The chaos, inequities, and callousness it offers are offset by a fundamental belief in designs hidden in its functioning.

LURE OF THE MYSTICAL

In addition to these unacknowleged nonsecular aspects, Vargas Llosa retains other nonrational elements in his moral theory. The *third* aspect of his moral theory has to do with his notion of daemons. Such a notion makes sense only as a vestige of a thoroughly nonsecular *Weltanschauung*. In a secular worldview, daemons would be conceived as drives or instincts, explainable in biological terms. As such, they would be seen as spurring us to action truly from beyond Good and Evil. Faced with such urges, the Few would embrace them as goods-in-themselves since their efficacy would coincide with their privilege. The Many would be terrified and would wish to return to the waiting arms of the church.

This was how Weber, following Nietzsche, understood the matter. Virile maturity would mean never returning to the arms of the church but pushing on, relying on power and cunning to survive in a world bereft of sure asymptotes for action. In such a world, survival would be utterly contingent. But it is worth remembering that Freud and Nietzsche, who claimed to have seen the human heart as it truly is, were both incapable of holding fast to their frightening discoveries. Ultimately, they both succumbed either to the lure of blind mystery or to the mystical. Vargas Llosa's daemons seem not to have a place in the world he wishes finally to embrace.

EMPIRICIST INSISTENCES

There is a fascinating empiricism in Vargas Llosa's thoughts on morality: he takes at face value a diffused feeling among his readers of sharing in a moral universe that is not clearly or exclusively based on religious feelings. He writes as if his readers had a tacit understanding of the truth of his theories, that such understanding could replace a clear articulation of his position. He takes it for granted, for example, that to disagree with the claim that there is such a thing as a secular morality, and that such a morality is rational and utilitarian, is tantamount to revealing a lack of acumen or civilized standing.

That a secular morality is feasible is far from being established beyond reasonable doubts. The Kantian effort to place reason as the ground of a moral universe failed in large part because (a) ultimately it could not dispense with God: the Godhead made possible the ethical commonwealth; and (b) a kernel of utilitarianism and hence heteronomy crept into its rational foundations. Durkheim's efforts, which began as a dual attack on Kantian rationalism and utilitarian thought, also failed. His reliance on Society as the indispensable God-term proved premature. The marxist effort failed in large part because, as Weber noted, it could not possibly answer key existential questions with its armoire of class-based categories. As for a utilitarian ground for moral systems, it is at least something that stands in need of defense. Kant's, Hegel's, and modern social theorists' efforts showing that both social and individual utilitarianism are inadequate to explain or ground a moral system cannot be easily dismissed. In fact, it could be argued that a secular morality is parasitic to a religious worldview.

BELIEVERS

There is a second aspect of Vargas Llosa's empiricism worth noting. He correctly observes that, by and large, the Many embrace the Godhead as their life-regulator. From there, and relying on a tacit appraisal of the inadequacy of religion to sustain modern life, he goes on to hold that the Many are not yet ready to adopt a virile posture.[2] In other words, he assumes his readers would all agree that to rely on a Godhead is a sign of tyronism. But what if one were to ask: what is wrong with holding the Godhead as the sole life-regulator? Why should those who believe in a deity be seen as somehow lacking in acumen or in virile maturity? The need for an articulated defense of such positions is quite clear.

There are no clearly articulated answers to these questions in Vargas Llosa's work. There are only intimations of possible answers. It seems, for example, that Vargas Llosa often falls back on the nineteenth-century notions of History and Reason to ground his views. No doubt such a tendency dates back to his days as a progressive marxist: since Humanity's advances show a unilinear, and hence an ever more unified, trajectory, eventually the plurality of deity-based moral systems will give way to one overarching secular moral system. In that scenario, Reason, now largely equated with Science, will take the place of God. Furthermore, and this is quite problematic, Reason will then demand a morality based on utility concerns. Lest we dismiss these views prematurely, we should note that, as with many of Marx's predictions, this sobering prediction appears to be coming true. It appears moral systems around the world are being eroded by the power of the Market as a giant calculus. As did Marx, Vargas Llosa celebrates the occurrence. But, clearly, perspicuity does not always mean correctness; rightness is not always reducible to success.

Is Marx's and Vargas Llosa's reading of history correct? Is it true that what undergirds postmodernity is a secular morality with utilitarian aims at its core? Perhaps. What must not be forgotten is that it is also an empirical occurrence, as Weber and Merton have shown, that the development of the market and of modern science was not only made possible by religion but also that these institutions continue to require traditional values to endure and to develop.[3] Minimally, therefore, the notion that the West (the Ideal Type of secularism, according to Vargas Llosa) has done away with religious values is in need of proof. It is certainly not the case in America, where the religious life of the Many is flourishing.[4] Whether the Few have abandoned such crutches altogether—never mind whether there are such individuals in the first place—is also in need of demonstration. On this issue, too, the long-taken-for-granted split between the Few and the Many is questionable.

GOING NATIVE

As with most anchoring visions, Vargas Llosa's image of the Western tradition is ideal-typical and utopic. In other words, he tends to magnify aspects of the West that he admires and to minimize those of which he disapproves. The psychological and theoretical feat does not seem to be extraordinary. First missionaries and then anthropologists claim to have already experienced and reflected on the matter for a long time. By their accounts, they seem to have been particularly susceptible to utopic thinking when they have ardently wished to be taken in by the

Other. Anthropologists classify this type of ideal-typical and utopic thinking as "going native."

Latin American history shows that the anticipatory acculturation involved in "going native" takes place in two directions. On the one hand, over the centuries, for example, many Europeans have forsworn their homeland and taken up residence among "primitive peoples" whom they have considered more truly human or genuine. On the other hand, many non-Westerners have feverishly embraced the culture of the West as the proper model to emulate. In view of the havoc caused on the Latin American cultural landscape by the Cultural Industry, it seems this process is far from over.

CONSERVATIVE CULTURES

As would be expected, it also happens that most natives, both in and outside the West, tend to love or admire their own cultures—as well they should, since they provide them with a place in the cosmos. As Durkheim, Weber, and Freud saw clearly, it is not always a bad thing to love oneself and one's people. Understandably, therefore, the natives would want to defend their culture against those who, influenced by the ways of the Other, point out obvious and not so obvious blemishes. In other words, all cultures are conservative at their core. The animosity shown by Americans against a T. S. Eliot or by Latin Americans against a Vargas Llosa exemplifies an expected nativistic defensiveness.

LOVE OF THE OTHER

"Going native" does not require a loss of all perspective. One could come to love or admire the ways of the Other and still not be blind to their shortcomings. Alternatively, one could come to love or admire the ways of the Other and not abandon love or respect for one's own culture. The case of Vargas Llosa is illustrative: over the years he has demonstrated awareness of some of the failures of capitalist postmodern societies and has shown some respect, if not straightforward love, for aspects of his native culture.[5]

Nor does "going native" require leaving land and home, never to return. On the contrary, it often involves a return, sometimes eagerly awaited, sometimes resisted. Those who immerse themselves among the Other often come back to tell the story and to describe the better ways of living and being they have found. It is a kind of redemption of the Other in the eyes of those who never left. "Going native" approximates, on a more thoroughly existential scale, the necessary transformation undergone by the would-be storytellers in Walter Benjamin's vision. As in the case of Benjamin's storytellers, the accounts of those who have "gone native" are necessarily part truth and part invention.[6]

PLUS PAPISTE QUE LE PAPE

As an invention, the stories of those who return are deeply affected by the ever-present rents and fissures in the faces of the Other. All such stories are a taking of sides. Consequently, in any given story, there is always a side among the aspects of the Other that is not told—or not told adequately. Only the eventual encounter between the two cultures, the two Others, can show the extent and the power of the different fissures and rents. The history of colonialism is a prime object-lesson of such occurrences.

It also happens that, after a fashion, those who began as neophyte guests among the Other come to believe themselves more knowledgeable about the ways of the Other than the Others themselves. They may even be bold enough to correct or chastise the "natives" for not living up to their Truth. They become *plus papiste que le Pape*.

THE WEST AS MYTH

Like most Peruvian intellectuals of his time, it seems Vargas Llosa went native well before he boarded the plane that took him to Paris, away from what he considered Peru's dismal milieu.[7] Once in the West, he took sides with particular groups of intellectuals: existentialist neomarxists at first, neoliberal ideologues later. Such groups were small and on the fringes of Western culture—taking the term in its broadest connotation. In time, like Benjamin's storytellers, Vargas Llosa became eager to return to Peru, with news of the ways of the West. Having gone native, however, his reports on the Other, in this case the ones Peruvians were to emulate, were expectedly biased and utopic.

As with all ideal-typical ideological positioning, Vargas Llosa's story strained for closure. In the long run, therefore, to maintain a cogent story line, he drew a conclusion: the partial and lingering failures of Western capitalist societies are the result of the natives' intransigencies, which act as impediments to the full realization of the Truth inherent in the Western way of life. Lately, Vargas Llosa has come to believe that the impediments are mostly the responsibility of the less advanced—and less virtuous—inhabitants of the West. He believes that some day, when capitalist societies are finally fully developed and all inhabitants are socialized to their ways, such impediments will be, if not eradicated, drastically curtailed.

Other neoliberals in the West see the matter differently. They often argue that such impediments are not at all native to their culture but are brought into the West by immigrants not civilized enough to sustain a rational and freely chosen market system. These immigrants, they hold, are full of chicanery: they are liars, cheats, corrupt, and beyond hope. The responsible thing to do, so as to implement fully the principles of neoliberalism and thus activate the creative powers of the Market, is to curtail such immigration.

There is an irony in all this: over the last few decades neoliberals have come to see Latin Americans, among other not fully integrated Westerners, very much as intellectuals like Vargas Llosa have portrayed them: morally corrupt and beyond redemption. In the end, neoliberals turn out to be one of Vargas Llosa's principal actual, as opposed to intended, sympathetic audiences. Surely against his wishes, Vargas Llosa fuels the xenophobic fires that, insofar as he is Peruvian, also lick at his heels.

MORAL/RELIGIOUS DIMENSIONS

The moral-religious residues from his original and adopted cultures allow Vargas Llosa to speak against the immorality of corruption, totalitarianism, interventionism, and, more recently, protectionism.[8] For a demonstration of the inefficiency of an economic system is never sufficient to support moral condemnation. Very much as Marx did, Vargas Llosa relies on traditional values, such as Justice, Fairness, and Charity, to buttress his arguments. Without such values, and in the absence of a new moral system, he is bereft of grounds to make moral judgments.[9]

RELIGIOUS COMPETITION

Vargas Llosa claims to be an agnostic and hence to hold no position regarding the existence or the nature of God.[10] He does understand, however, the uses of religion as a social institution. Without its rule-enforcing and will-bending force, he holds, societies around the world would be in peril. This utilitarian understanding of religion is based on a conception of the different religions as so many cultural products in the social inventory of institutions, value systems, and worldviews. This available variety, product of the historically ever more complex competition of ideas, he believes, is something that ought to be protected, so long as it is needed by the Many. In fact, Vargas Llosa advocates a free and hence healthy competition for the souls of believers—until the time comes when no such crutches will be necessary.

In this context, Vargas Llosa welcomes the growth of the Protestant churches in Latin America. Due to its long monopoly over the fears and dreams of the Many, without an effective competition from advanced religious institutions from the West, Vargas Llosa claims, the Catholic Church there has become lethargic and complacent. The latest attempt by the faithful to renew it from within—exemplified by the efforts of Liberation Theologians—is destined to fail so long as its monopoly is maintained.[11] Only competition from other advanced religious institutions, not animism or a rapprochement with the materialist tradition, will provide the necessary renewal of the Catholic Church in Latin America.

RELIGION AND CIVIL SOCIETY

The notion of religious competition within a posited neoliberal society is predicated on the return to a very old conception of Civil Society with its clear separation between private and public spheres. In this conception, as in the case of the acquisitions of other goods in the market, the choice of gods and churches must be kept as a private affair; it must be seen as a matter or personal taste and not of social obligation. In this sense, Vargas Llosa goes way back, past Marx, to take sides with the Young Hegelians.[12] But, since then, the marxist critique of religion first, and the sociology of religion later, have made plain that the attempt to separate private and public spheres is chimerical.

This is an example of Vargas Llosa's utopic story concerning the West. He tends to second-guess the natives, for it must be clear, to anyone who has looked into the matter with care, that the separation of private and public spheres in America and Europe has never been as clear-cut as he often makes it out to be. This fact is acknowledged and used by a growing numbers of American and European neoliberals who, over the last few decades, have been trying to develop ever closer ties between Christianity and the State.

The deep and inevitable relationship between private and public spheres must have been even more palpable to Vargas Llosa in his old homeland. When he was running for president there, perhaps with second thoughts, he acquiesced in using the Catholic Church's influence among the Many for his own political ends.[13] Since his political defeat, Vargas Llosa has even shown willingness to draw closer to his religious roots.[14] Were he to continue in that direction, he might end up embracing some form of religiosity. The change of heart would not be unprecedented. It has been quite common among neoliberals the world over.

PRIVILEGED INTELLECTUALS

His appreciation of the need for regulation notwithstanding, Vargas Llosa wishes to defend the right of individuals to violate the norms of society. They are enjoined to follow their daemons and their dreams. But, as we have seen, it is also his position that not all individuals are, or ought to be, equally obligated to live up to their own dimly felt expectations. Most, in fact, must toil within the safe parameters of clear valuations. Only the Few can face the world devoid of illusions. Artists, those urged by their daemons to give form and expression to their dreams, he holds, ought in particular to be exempt from the necessary moral/religious prescriptions and proscriptions. To pursue the Good Lie is their daemon-commanded duty. In this sense, Vargas Llosa continues the Latin American tradition, in large part inherited from Europe, that accords intellectuals, artists in particular, a privileged status.[15] But he extends and contracts the tradition in specific ways.

The Extension

Whereas the Latin American tradition imbues the position of intellectuals with a quasi-religious aura and presents them as wise Truthtellers who bear counsel concerning the Good Life, Vargas Llosa's notions seem to draw us closer to the Nietzschean Good Europeans: virilely mature individuals include those intellectuals who behold the world free from illusions and walk among us pointing out our failings and dispelling illusions with laughter or irony, but always with a Truthtelling animus.

This extension, if true, poses some difficulties not fully discussed by Vargas Llosa: if the quasi-religious aura no longer envelops these artists, if, in fact, the religious itself is questioned by their work, why should society—the Many—continue to accord intellectuals a privileged status? Why should they be exempt from the moral demands to which the Many are subjected? Stripped of such a quasi-religious aura, who are these "artists" in the first place? A tacit understanding of such privilege is not readily available outside cultures like that of Latin America, so suffused as they are with the religious. After Kant and the death of aesthetics, it is not clear that even members of the secular Western cultural elite are in agreement as to the nature and value of the artistic vision.

In the absence of an articulated answer to these questions, we are left to guess at a possible response: since Vargas Llosa believes that identities and ideas, like all other goods in the capitalist cultural inventory, are best nurtured and developed in the free exchanges taking place in the marketplace, perhaps we come to know we are in the presence of an artist when he is successful in the market. In this scenario, the objective culling process of the market would determine who is an artist and we would then know to whom we should accord a privileged position.

The Contraction

The following critique is applicable to all of Latin America, but particularly to the case of Peru. When he was young, Vargas Llosa tells us, he believed in the traditional Peruvian image of the intellectual: intellectuals constituted a kind of moral reserve in a land of immorality; they were bearers of ideals against an oppressive reality. In time, however, he came to realize that such was not the case. Entirely to the contrary. Intellectuals turned out to be among the most immoral of Peruvians. They are easily enticed with material rewards or intimidated with loss of prestige or power.[16] Indeed, he bemoans the fact that some Peruvian writers are ready to forswear their calling for the sake of psychological or material rewards. Others prostitute their ideals for the sake of survival. Under these conditions, the writer who, like Vargas Llosa himself, stays true to his calling cannot but become the target of envious attacks. As a response, writers like Vargas Llosa become moralists. Even politics, in the hands of such writers, becomes a moral enterprise. In short, according to Vargas Llosa, the entire effort of the Peruvian writer must be geared toward a moral regeneration.[17]

MORAL REGENERATION

As the politico/artist descends among the Many, what sort of moral regeneration will he demand? Vargas Llosa does not wish to bid his audience, as some earlier writer/critics have done, to return to the ancient, truer, or more humane cultural roots of Peru. Nor does he wish to propose a new — that is, a mestizo — culture.[18] The obvious answer is that the demand will be for Peruvians to become ever more European. On this Vargas Llosa joins legions of Latin American intellectuals who have seen the whitening of their continent as the only salvation from barbarism.[19] However, if we are to believe him, to become European means to be free from injunctions based on traditional and primitive worldviews. Why should the Many heed his call for regeneration? And would it lead us to a better, more just, and more integrated world? Or would it instead bring us closer to the chaos, relativism, and nihilism that the Good Europeans celebrate and thus put fear into our hearts?

THE FICTION WRITER

The fundamental ambivalence in Vargas Llosa's position regarding the moral order and the individual's response is most clearly appreciated in the relationship he sees between Society and the writer of fiction. On the one hand, he argues that the novel flourishes in times when morals are being questioned and belief systems are in crisis. He follows Lukacs in believing that there is a kind of amorality and skepticism at the core of the novel. And yet, on the other hand, he wishes to hold that just because the novel attacks the established moral order does not mean that it itself is not moral. On the contrary. The great novel, he observes, displays a deeply moral component.[20]

How to defend the transgressing nature of the novel while, at the same time, expecting it to be moral? It could be done in at least two ways: first, by seeing the novel as a vehicle for the articulation of traditional values, which have been misunderstood or forgotten by the Many or the powers that be. In this case, Vargas Llosa would be continuing the traditional role of the writer in Latin America who saw his art as tools for regeneration. Or, second, by seeing the novel as the vehicle for the re-presentation of a new morality. In this case the writer of fiction would be following Nietzsche's lead: art, philosophy, and cultural leadership coincide. In either of these cases, the grounds for the moral stance of the writer would be more or less clear. So far, however, Vargas Llosa does not seem to have opted for either of these ways of reconciliation; nor has he articulated an alternative.

MARKETS AND MORALS

Vargas Llosa defends the free play of the individual's desires while accepting that without rules freedom is not possible; for even a well-functioning and self-regulated market requires that certain rules be obeyed.[21] He resolves this apparent contradiction by holding that in a free market the necessary rules are self-given and not imposed by the State or any other regulatory agency. Reasonable individuals entering the market will naturally come to the conclusion that to obey such enabling rules is the best way to obtain freedom. Self-interest makes freedom possible.

This belief is problematic. In the first place, it suffers from the shortcoming of all contract theories: why would already privileged and powerful individuals forgo their interests (and all at once) to enter the free market on an equal basis? Let us recall that this was one reason why Marx argued that revolution was necessary. In the second place, it suffers from all the shortcomings of utilitarian foundations for rules, which is best shown by its total inability to respond to Glaucon's challenge: why should anyone who is sure he will not be caught obey any rule whatsoever?

5

Civilization and Barbarism

In our dreams images represent the sensations we think they cause; we do not feel horror because we are threatened by a sphinx; we dream of a sphinx in order to explain the horror we feel.

—J. L. Borges, after Coleridge

AESTHETIC TENDENCIES

The animus of the Total Novel, argues Vargas Llosa, is to represent the Evil side of humanity. Such Evil has at least two sides, or moments: it is something labeled as such and repressed by Society, and something ready at hand and in need of curtailment. The first side concerns Society's proscriptions of individual desires. In that case, the animus of art is to give voice to the repressed urges. The second aspect concerns concrete social practices that go against such values as Justice and Freedom. In this case the animus of art is, through an aesthetic depiction, to denounce these practices. In both cases, the aesthetic vision kindles the fires of social change.

Vargas Llosa differs from postmodernist writers on this point. He believes art has something important to say with respect to both moments of Evil. He continues to be an engaged intellectual and hence still believes there is a Good to be upheld. He wishes to keep such valuations as background for his art, to be sure. They are not to become the raison d'être of the aesthetic effort. He has even proposed that writers ought to more properly address such concerns in nonliterary works, which is something he himself has done. But he must also know that it is ultimately impossible to keep art and social theory separate. The Truthtelling effort suffuses the writer/critic. All art is tendentious.

CIVILIZACIÓN Y BARBARIE

The animus of his Total Novel has led Vargas Llosa to describe Peru as a place of Evil, a corrupt and oppressive society. In his fiction and other writing, he illustrates such Evil through the prisms of class, race, gender, bad institutions, and warped personalities. In this sense, Vargas Llosa follows in the footsteps of earlier Latin American and especially Peruvian writer/critics—even as his valuations are deftly woven in highly accomplished aesthetic forms.

But Evil does not exist without its opposite. As with Lying and Truthtelling, if there is no Good, there is no Evil, and vice versa. Given this truism, where does Vargas Llosa locate the Good that exists in the context of Latin America in general and Peru in particular? Not surprisingly, keeping in mind Vargas Llosa's ideal-typical and utopic image of the West, he locates Good in the Western way of life that manages to exist there, weak and on the run.

From this starting position, Vargas Llosa continues in the Latin American tradition when he gathers all these manifestations of Good and Evil into one overarching trope: Latin America in general and Peru in particular are equipoised between Civilization and Barbarism. And having attained such an insight, like most modern writer/critics, he rises to defend Civilization and to put his shoulder against Barbarism. He is undeterred by the complications attending his heroic gesture: in a postmodern world, where traditional Western values are not easily afforded privileged status, it is increasingly difficult to make easy distinctions between the Civilized and the Barbarous.[1] Those nineteenth-century valuations are tattered and perhaps beyond repair.

FACUNDO

The clearest statement of the Civilization and Barbarism divide was made in the nineteenth century. In 1845 Domingo F. Sarmiento published his famous *Facundo*, a book in which he presented Argentina in particular, but Latin America as a whole, with the choice of embracing either Europe (Civilization) or mestizo America (Barbarism). The book soon became a rallying symbol for Europeans and europhiles across the barbarous land.[2] But, of course, others had already claimed to have made the scandalous choice. In fact, at the very inception of Latin America, the trope helped to justify genocide, since barbarism was then synonymous with heathen, Indian, and American. Having encountered different conceptions of life and the cosmos, the overzealous representatives of Western culture came to believe that, for their own sake, the natives had to be "civilized" at all costs. The mestizo was the inevitable outcome of the white man's civilizing deed in a barbarous land.

The "civilizing" deed was nearly unquestioned for three hundred years, until the beginning of the nineteenth century when, during the wars of independence, civilized men leading barbarians restated the original choice. In fact, Bolivar believed the choice involved the very existence of a truly American civilization. But his efforts were not enough to make his dream of a Latin American Nation a reality. Then, by the middle of this century, marxists claimed to have the liberation of the Many in mind, as they attacked the greed of the civilized classes. They then talked about a New Man for a new, socialist civilization. Their efforts were also derailed. And now, in the last quarter of the twentieth century, a small group of neoliberals claim to be the new spokesmen for the barbarians. In truth, they claim, the Many fervently wish to participate in the universal culture made possible by capitalism. Marx was right up to a point: the market system is proving that there is one way of leading a civilized life—the Western way.

DARKEST PERU

In his literary works, Vargas Llosa represents Peru as a barbarous land. The Many are often portrayed as nearly subhuman beings, heirs to the blemishes proper to the primitive cultures of Indians, blacks, Asians, and mestizos. Some Indian cultures are conceived as outside of human history altogether. Afro-Peruvians are portrayed as naked savages. Asian Peruvians are seen as devious and inscrutable. Mestizos appear as a motley mass of tormentors and victims.[3]

Vargas Llosa seems to be caught in the same manicheistic thinking prevalent among the Indigenista and socialist writers whom he often criticizes. He also seems to divide Peru into two irreconcilable camps, only with reverse valuations. In reality, however, he must be even more radical: the contrasting pole to Barbarism is not to be found in Peru at all. He wants to show that the history of Peru can be best appreciated as the unfolding of the conquerors' not civilizing but barbarous deed. All Peruvians are stained by the barbarism from the beginning. The low-class, uneducated, ruthless, conniving conquerors, it turns out, were not true representatives of the Western peoples. It is no accident, therefore, that there is hardly a "civilized" Peruvian portrayed in his literary works. Civilization, as Vargas Llosa conceives of it, could only be represented by a mythical and ever more enlightened Europe.

PESSIMISM, TRUTH, AND THE EXOTIC

It could be that this understanding is not fair to Vargas Llosa. In particular, it could be that, if the distinction between author and narrator is kept in mind, his different characters represent an attempt to achieve the Total Novel, to release the Truth through the Good Lie. But it is precisely because of Vargas Llosa's notion regarding the Total Novel that the Truth of his art is problematic. First of all, if we are to take the notion of a Total Novel seriously, we should expect the author to attempt to give adequate voice at least to a modicum of complementary characters in Peruvian reality, since the aim is to grasp its complexity in one aesthetic vision. The author does not provide these complementary characters. There are hardly any characters who illustrate the standpoint of the other Peruvians: those not condemned to utter depravity and suffering. Vargas Llosa's Truth is overly pessimistic.

It is not only his aesthetic insights that undergird his one-sided and pessimistic portrayal of Peruvians. His sociopolitical writings are a veritable defense of this *maudit* view of Peruvian history. In fact, if we are to take seriously his theories concerning daemons, we must acknowledge that the characters and voices he chooses to represent Peruvian reality do indeed obey the power of his personal, historical, and cultural daemons.[4] This means that, following his overall theories concerning social and political matters, his one-sided views on Peru are meant to be discussed in the free market of ideas. They gain particular value when they serve to counter the overly optimistic official story of would-be heroes and their deeds. This means the appraisal of the aesthetic insight cannot be contained within an aesthetic discourse.

A TOURIST IN HIS OWN LAND

One might observe that, because of his limited sociocultural background, Vargas Llosa does not really know most Peruvians. When it comes to non-Westerners, one could argue, his views are as touristic as were those of many Indigenista writers in the early part of the century.[5] And, indeed, his sporadic trips to the Amazon and Andean regions can hardly be seen as sufficient to provide him with a deep understanding of the people living there. By his own account, he does not speak their language or understand their worldviews. Under such conditions, he is liable to perpetuate unjust clichés and stereotypes.

Vargas Llosa has spent more time in Madrid or London than in the Andes, for example. And yet, so far he has not written fiction based on such experiences. Is it because he expects, as did anthropologists until very recently, that the natives of Peru will not speak back and therefore he can proclaim himself an expert on their ways? It would seem not. His critics in Peru and abroad have been quite severe. Rather, he believes his years in Peru and his acquaintance with Peruvians who do know and are affected by the so-called primitive cultures are warrant enough. It is not surprising, therefore, that the so-called primitives in his literature are always seen through the eyes of mestizos or whites. There is an absence of complex non-Western characters in his oeuvre. In short, Vargas Llosa's Total Novel is the aesthetic vision of a europhile mestizo that presupposes the sublation or marginalization of the so-called primitives.

(It is interesting to note that the aesthetic vision of the primitive is appealing to Vargas Llosa's readers, particularly those outside Latin America. It plays on the old dichotomy of Civilization and Barbarism so prevalent in the nineteenth-century colonial literature. In Vargas Llosa's works, Western readers find themselves reassured in their belief in the superiority of their culture; while the so-called primitives are represented as that side of humanity that needs to be left behind. Vargas Llosa's work is a marvelous addition to the long line of cultural products sold as exotica.)

PATERNALISM

Since Vargas Llosa sees himself as a representative of Civilization in the midst of Barbarism, the disclosure of injustice is often done from a paternalistic perspective. He seldom sees the evil deeds of the Many as conscious or willful events. The Many are mostly portrayed as merely trying to survive in an evil world, obeying atavistic and primitive conceptions of life and the cosmos, or reacting to the evil actions of the Civilized, who ought to know better. The paternalistic attitude is particularly salient when it comes to the so-called primitives: it is not their fault if they act like animals; they have been abandoned in their barbarous state by those who ought to have saved them.[6] This paternalistic view makes it almost imperative that the so-called primitives be represented in his literature as an anonymous mass or through a series of worn-out stereotypes.

As might be expected, this paternalistic attitude is the basis of Vargas Llosa's acid critique of those Peruvians who ought to know better. There indeed is a strong moral component in many of Vargas Llosa's works. That barbarous acts would be committed by the Many can be explained as consequences of underdevelopment. That the so-called Civilized would engage in evil acts such as repression or corruption is inexcusable. In doing so, they only contribute to the notion around the world that *all* Peruvians are barbarians. They also abrogate their responsibility of elevating the Many to the level of the civilized.

RACISM AND CLASSISM

Vargas Llosa is not a racist. He does not believe, as did Borges, that Indians, blacks, or Asians are inferior to whites.[7] Nor does he maintain that the so-called primitives have no culture. On the contrary, he believes they have internalized values and ways of being that they share as a group.[8] As did most nineteenth-century social theorists, though, he maintains that, among the multiplicity of cultures extant around the world, there are some that stand evolutionarily higher. And, of course, at the highest level of development we find Western cultures. Furthermore, as we have seen, he believes that within Western cultures there exists an inescapable distinction between the Few and the Many. In other words, Vargas Llosa can be more properly understood as a cultural ethnocentrist (Western, not Peruvian) and a classist.

The distinction is crucial. Like all modern social theorists, Vargas Llosa firmly believes that all human beings share in the important dimensions of their being. It is possible and desirable, therefore, that the distinction between Civilization and Barbarism be overcome through action, in time. There are no biological barriers to the possibility of all humans eventually attaining the Good Society and the Good Life. In fact, Vargas Llosa has added more recently, now that the Market has shown its worth in the face of the totalitarian experiments of this century, it is only a matter of time before all humanity shares in the wealth that only the Market can generate. To believe that Peruvians are incapable of succeeding in the marketplace, or that they ought to be protected from the salutary effects of free competition, or that they should be helped to find other ways of organizing their society rather than capitalism, he argues, is truly a racist argument. The only thing preventing the Peruvian Many from being fully civilized is their attachment to the dross of their non-Western traditions.[9]

IDENTITY AND SOCIETY

The roots of the colonial mentality exhibited by Vargas Llosa lead back to the very beginning of Latin American history. In the case of Peru, the issue was clearly restated by Salazar Bondy during the middle of the twentieth century. He noted that, for centuries, the Peruvian elite had been in the clutches of what Raúl Barrenechea had described as "something like a misplaced nostalgia."[10] It was a nostalgia for a colonial splendor that, if it was ever real, had been lost to the heirs of the conquerors by his time. For his part, José Carlos Mariátegui had noted that members of the national elite had never felt Peruvian, but rather believed themselves to be Spaniards living in a land conquered by Spain for their benefit.[11] We can see that Vargas Llosa has provided a new and improved version of that nostalgia: if we could only be Europeans.

RETREATING WOULD-BE EUROPEANS

Until the middle of this century, the national elites managed to overcome all resistance to their claim that they embodied the Peruvian identity.[12] Not even Indigenismo could shake their ideological hold on the nation. At bottom, they claimed, all Peruvians wished to be European—and hence imitate the imitators. Their claims only began to ring hollow during the great rural to urban migration of the midcentury. Indians and mestizos began then to claim spaces in the urban centers previously reserved for white and whitening Europeans. It was during this period that Lima was first surrounded and then overtaken by non-Europeans.

Members of the elite then either fled abroad or hid in compounds behind barbed wire, electric fences, and steel gates.

This transformation of Lima and other coastal urban centers was accompanied by a reformulation of the ideological skirmishes waged for the Peruvian identity. By the sixties and seventies, but particularly during the eighties, the traditional claim to cultural hegemony by Europe was being challenged by an aggressive Cultural Industry stemming initially from the United States and later from a global economy. At that time, dazzled by the short-term economic performance of supply-side economics, intellectuals like Vargas Llosa repeated a harangue once heard at the end of the nineteenth century: let us embrace the Protestant values of England and America.[13] All this coincided with the collapse of the socialist economies and the ascendancy of Freedom over Justice as the master-category of social theory.

The replacement of Spain as the cultural home of Latin Americans was already begun in the nineteenth century. There were two distinctive tendencies among the cultured elite then: one followed the lead of Catholic France, the other that of Protestant America. In Peru, because of the central role Lima played during the colonial period, these tendencies were not as pronounced. Peruvians were Catholic: they had the saints and the Inquisition to prove it. Still, by the end of World War II, the dream of most Peruvian intellectuals was to go to Paris. Vargas Llosa was not atypical in seeing French culture as the culture of high class and sophistication. By the fifties, it served as a distinctive and effective marker for the distinction between the Few and the Many.[14] By the eighties, as he embraced neoliberalism, Vargas Llosa swung to the other tendency present in the nineteenth century: he came to admire the WASP values of Ronald Reagan and Margaret Thatcher.

HUACHAFOS

Up until the development of the Cultural Industry over the last three decades, the appropriation of imported cultural markers had been the prerogative of the Peruvian Few. As is to be expected in neocolonial societies, the elites were more than reluctant to share such markers with the Many. The distinction was necessary to maintain ideological and economic control. The arrival of the Cultural Industry signaled a transformation in the patterns of acquisition of these markers. Phenotypical characteristics and prior cultural capital became less important as passwords in the new world of gadgets and degrees. Except in tiny, isolated enclaves, money began replacing all earlier tokens of inclusion. The term *huachafo*, which was coined in the first decades of the century, expressed the elite's desire to develop alternative markers to maintain invidious distinctions. Immigrants with capital but no "taste" or "manners" were dismissed as *huachafos*. Mestizos trying to pass for European were, and are, considered *huachafos*.[15]

THE LAST CULTURE ON EARTH

The culture of the "Civilized" in Latin America has changed over the years. The Spanish claim lasted more than three hundred years; that of the French at least a century. As the American century comes to a close, it is hard to tell what culture, if any, will endure as a recognizable and integrating worldview of the future. Perhaps Weber was right: the capitalist nullity might go on believing that it has created the greatest and last culture on earth.

As far as Latin America is concerned, there is no question that the cultural elites will continue to tie their fate to that of the West.[16] Whatever contribution Latin Americans can make to the world at large, they heartily believe, it will come as an extension of Western culture.[17] Perhaps Vargas Llosa is right: the culture of the Barbarians—now scattered in shanty towns, plazas, main streets, brothels, and fields—has no place in the future of the continent.[18] Vargas Llosa's vision, which coincides with the general appraisal, is as disturbing as it is honest.

6

Politics and Literature

In our wildest aberrations we dream of an equilibrium we have left behind and which we naively expect to find at the end of our errors.

—A. Camus

USES OF UTOPIA

It is by now axiomatic that biographical and social sediments intrude in all literary production. At least in the realm of arts and letters the pretense of objectivity has never been taken too seriously. In consonance with the accepted truism, Vargas Llosa tells us that the Truthtelling task of the writer is necessarily informed by personal and social daemons. He further intimates that these daemons often coincide in their demands and that to understand one is to understand the other. This coincidence functions as a leitmotif in one of his best novels, *Conversación en La Catedral*, in which Santiago Zavala, the main character, wonders exactly when Peru went to hell. In his increasing drunken stupor, the young man understands that his self-understanding and personal salvation hinge on his understanding of Peruvian history.

A GOLDEN AGE

At what moment did Peru really go to hell? The question presupposes that there was a time when the poor country faced heaven. Scoffers like Salazar Bondy might even say that it presupposes a dreamy, utopian past, an invented golden age before

51

the debacle. Such scoffers know, of course, that the presupposition, though false, was never altogether innocuous. On the contrary, a utopian past has been held up, again and again, since before the fateful encounter between Europe and America, as a useful gloss for the claim of hegemony of different groups ruling the poor land.

In its effects, the presupposition of a golden age has alternated like the two faces of Ometeotl.[1] At times, it has spurred humans into action to pursue a better future. This was the case during the wars of independence and during the guerrilla wars of this century. At times, it has served as a soothing opiate. In such cases, a retreat to a dreamy past has replaced action in the present. Salazar Bondy's critique shows this most clearly.

PROFFERED UTOPIAS

The dream of a utopic past has had its counterpart in the dreams of a utopic future. The claims to hegemony by succeeding ruling groups, we must admit, have always been paired, embellished, with dreams of a utopic future. America itself, as Edmundo O'Gorman has pointed out, began as such a utopic invention. Of course, the intellectual and spiritual invention soon mixed with the deeds of conquest, and greed edged out salvation. In Peru since the conquest, there have been several proffered utopias, all sustained by the succeeding spikes of wealth: the gold boom, the rubber boom, the copper boom, the fish meal boom, the cocaine boom. For those who profited, each spike of wealth left traces of what could have been. Peruvians had reasons for nostalgia. More generally, Vargas Llosa points out, Peruvians exhibit a tendency to embrace the utopic at the expense of the feasible.

AN OPPRESSIVE PRESENT

When did Peru really go to hell? It depends on who answers the question. Santiago Zavala, scion of a wealthy and traditional family, cannot find an easy answer. His personal hell—love and hatred for a homosexual father, love and resentment for a suppliant mother, respect and desire for the *niñas bien*—fuses with the hellish corruption of the world around him. For Santiago Zavala there is no utopia, neither in the past nor in the future. He is destined to live in an eternal, oppressive present. In this he is paradigmatic of most of Vargas Llosa's characters.

PREPARATORY UTOPIA

The image of a utopic past has always been present in Peruvian literature. One of its earliest instances was offered by Inca Garcilaso de la Vega. In his *Comentarios reales* the mestizo writer accepts the supremacy of the Spanish Crown and presents the world of his mother as an already surpassed, if preparatory, utopia. The image of a golden age was then used as an apologetics. During the republican period, and until very recently, the whites and mestizos of Lima maintained the myth of the colonial period as a golden age in their stories, poetry, and songs. Utopia served then, Salazar Bondy pointed out, as a soothing opiate. Then, during the first decades of this century, Garcilaso de la Vega's utopia was resurrected. As a socioliterary movement, Indigenismo attempted to fuse the image of a utopic past with a protest against present conditions. As Vargas Llosa notes, José María Arguedas exemplifies this attempt most clearly. He invented an Indian culture based on the materials he collected from the real Peru.

DISTOPIA AND SOCIAL THEORY

As writer and critic, Vargas Llosa wishes to distance himself from such utopias. To him, there never was a golden age; neither before nor after the conquest. Before the conquest there existed in the Andes a totalitarian, barbaric State. The colonial period was an improvement; but it was never free from the cobwebs of ignorance and beatitude. Therefore, the Peruvian past, especially the official past, is nothing but a trail of deception and simulation. Against such a tendency toward utopian thinking, Vargas Llosa proposes a realist thinking, guided by Reason, Science, and ruthless Truthtelling.

No, Santiago Zavala does not have a utopian image to afford him respite from the oppressive present, a present seen as the result of countless false starts and compulsive repetitions. Rather, he lives in a distopia. His world is utterly corrupt and corrupting, and his present does not nurture authenticity.[2] But, of course, this is Vargas Llosa's own myth. In trying to escape the lure of mythology, he has ended up inventing a world without hope, utterly oppressive and utterly unreal. He might be absolutely honest in his portrayal of Peruvian society; but honesty is no guarantee of truth; it speaks only to good intentions.

THE MARKET AND UTOPIA

The mythmaking effort in his literature makes sense when we consider Vargas Llosa's work as a social theorist. As he has embraced neoliberalism with ever more determination, he has imbued his Will to Truth, like his Will to Power, with utopic elements. His utopia, which he defends as a realist stance and scientific Truth, is a modern capitalism grounded on a smoothly functioning Market. In his neoliberal ideology, the Market is posited as the necessary mechanism for the overcoming of the antinomies of Duty and Desire, Individual and Society. In this sense, the hellish present represented in literature is preparatory to embracing the utopic future prefigured in his social theory.

THE APOCALYPSE: THEORY AND FICTION

There has always been a sense of doom hovering in the Latin American novel. Octavio Paz attributes it to the nature of the novel itself, since it is like an acid that corrodes the social fabric. In Vargas Llosa's literary theory, it could be conceived as the writer's penchant for letting the Evil, repressed side of humanity have its say. Be that as it may, it is clear that Latin American literature has always represented a society fated to exist either at the brink of disaster or on this side of a portentous new beginning. In Vargas Llosa's novels, particularly some of the more recent ones, that sense of doom has taken a radical turn: it has become apocalyptic. Why?

By his own account, Vargas Llosa was never a true marxist and never wished to write a "tendentious" novel in the social-realist mode. But he was perhaps sufficiently influenced by marxist theories to accept that, if there is to be salvation from a hellish present, it has to come as a result of collective action. The insight is crucial. For, surveying his homeland, since the fifties, he sees a community without prospects of salvation. He sees its collective will floundering in simulation and self-deception. Evil appears to have settled there for all eternity. In the absence of willful collective action to change things, Vargas Llosa surmises, the writer is left with the task of telling the Truth: Peru, that land the color of excrement, is a damned place where classes and races cannot stand each other.[3] The Truthtelling effort produced the notion of a Total Novel. But decades of continued struggles and disappointments appear to have taken their toll. As barbarians from the countryside (with their bad smells, duplicitous alliances, and aggressive poverty) and barbarians from the city (misguided, merciless, brutal guerrillas) began choking the meager civilization radiating from the centers of coastal cities, the prospects for salvation receded so much that the conclusion was inevitable: apocalypse awaits.

In Vargas Llosa's literature, apocalypse threatens at the moment when chaos and power coincide. In and of itself, power can be will-bending and life-regulating. As Nietzsche was fond of noting, even naked power could manage to harness the energy of the Many to enhance civilization. In Peru, Vargas Llosa shows in his novels, power was able to sustain the often cruel and immoral but civilizing steadiness of class distinctions, residential segregation, racial inequalities, and gender delineations. When those distinctions are done away with, when power exists in a world in chaos, as in the contemporary Peru of Vargas Llosa's vision, power becomes shifting, destructive; it loses even the meager benefit that justified it.[4]

TONTOS Y VIVOS

In such times, everything becomes a matter of survival. The social world turns manicheistic: the *vivos* will survive; the *tontos* will perish. Ironically, the

Truthtelling effort of Vargas Llosa ends up where he claims the efforts of his naive predecessors also ended. But, there is a crucial difference: In Vargas Llosa's postmodernist novels, the writer/god stands aloof from his creation; he does not offer guiding valuations. Good and Evil, *vivos* and *tontos*, are merely descriptive categories.[5]

Still, *vivos* and *tontos* must make choices. The idea that bad institutions could thwart the human will beyond recognition is not acceptable to Vargas Llosa. But the choices are limited. Reading his novels, it appears Peruvians might be able to choose from among the following options: (a) become a *vivo*, aggressively; (b) accept being a *tonto*; (c) withdraw from the public into a private world; (d) move from one world to another; and (e) rebel—against all odds.

OPTIONS

Whites and whitening mestizos pursue the first option. Their position in society affords them a modicum of success. They are better prepared to simulate and dissimulate to take advantage of opportunities.[6] The second is the option of the Many. Women resign themselves to making peace with a machista world. Blacks, Indians, and homosexuals find survival at all costs the only option. The third option is taken up by those wealthy enough or deranged enough to retreat to a private world.[7] The fourth option involves not only a mental but a physical exile.[8] Finally, there is always the possibility of rebellion. But, heeding the realist element in his calling, Vargas Llosa portrays all rebellion as doomed to failure. In Peru, he tells us, revolutionary leaders are inevitably naive, resentful, or cruel. Overall, the violence unleashed by rebellion ends up dashing the hopes of guilty and innocent alike.[9]

OPEN AND CLOSED SOCIETIES

In the sixties, Vargas Llosa was a supporter of armed struggle against what was then called the Peruvian bourgeois state. Like most other left-wing intellectuals, he then believed that in order to bring about a more just society in Peru, it was necessary to replace the prevalent capitalist economic formations with socialist practices.[10] The influence of Jean-Paul Sartre's brand of existential marxism on Vargas Llosa's politics and social philosophy was decidedly strong. He wrote then that he had no desire to traffic with what Albert Camus had called the "philosophy of the just."[11] It was to take many years before he came around to reappraising Camus's position and to feeling free from the ghost of Jean-Paul Sartre, the mandarin.

Given his career as a writer/critic, Vargas Llosa has always been sensitive to the rights of the individual. No doubt, he embraced Sartre's brand of socialism at least in part because it made adequate room for individual choice. And yet, despite such sensitivity, or perhaps because of it, he kept a central tenet of socialist thought in his philosophical outlook for years: individualism is something to be looked at askance. Even during the mid-eighties, as he embraced aggressive neoliberal social theories, he continued to appreciate the need of Society to exact a life-enhancing compliance from individuals.[12] He seems to have been keenly aware of Marx's gloss on the antinomy of Individual and Society: only in community can the individual flourish. He even saw justifications for the State to intervene in Civil Society.[13] In short, by the mid-eighties Vargas Llosa still believed the reconciliation of individual and society could only be achieved by striking a balance between two irreconcilable goods.[14]

Many years after becoming increasingly disillusioned by the socialist experiments around the world, Vargas Llosa still managed to articulate support for a type of socialism that pursued Justice, but not at the expense of certain bourgeois freedoms, such as freedom of the press.[15] His steadily weakening support for the Cuban revolution was based on that articulation. It proved tenuous in the long run, of course. By the nineties, Vargas Llosa followed Karl Popper in dividing societies into two camps: open and closed. Closed societies could be a product of left or right politics. In the context of Latin America, such societies were exemplified by Cuba on the left and Pinochet's dictatorship on the right.

EVIL IN POLITICS

In the last decade, Vargas Llosa's aversion for all types of socialist thinking has become visceral. His uncompromising position may have been influenced, at least to some degree, by all-too-human factors, such as personal friendships, betrayals, likes and dislikes. But there seems to be something more involved in his aversion. Like Ronald Reagan, for example, Vargas Llosa often speaks of closed societies as the product of something Evil, something that precedes and outlives its particular manifestations.

For him there seem to be two particularly Evil aspects of socialist thinking. First, in a notion that approximates Freud's conception of the death instinct—which strives toward ultimate rest—Vargas Llosa believes there is a force in the depths of humanity that surfaces now and again seeking uniformity and aiming to destroy what is different, unplanned, and new. Second, and closely related to the first, there is a recurrent desire to fuse fiction and reality.[16] The effort to implant an ideal, fictive uniformity, in the case of socialism through a planned economy and society, he claims, has caused much suffering throughout the ages.

It is important to reiterate in this context that, again much like Freud, Vargas Llosa understands these aspects of Evil as antipodes to other deep-seated urges in the human heart: urges to give in to chaos and nihilism. He does not advocate radical freedom. On the contrary, he has always distanced himself from the radical positions taken by some postmodern theorists—such as Lacan or Derrida—which he suspects are fraudulent.[17] Rather, he wants to steer free from the Scylla of order and the Charybdis of chaos. He wishes to find a resting place to end his oscillations. It is in this context that he embraces neoliberalism, the philosophy of measured freedoms and responsibilities.

FREEDOM AND JUSTICE

The neoliberal position is invested by Vargas Llosa with the power to solve the fundamental antinomies of modern society. In particular, he sees it as the only realistic way to solve what Talcott Parsons, that great conservative sociologist, called the problem of order.[18] In the context of Vargas Llosa's political concerns, neoliberalism was seen as the best way to address the problems associated with the relationship between Justice and Freedom. For it seemed clear to him that, in drifting toward a closed society, Cuba had chosen Justice over Freedom.

The choice was mistaken. Correctly understood, Vargas Llosa points out, Freedom does not preclude Justice. On the contrary, only in Freedom is Justice possible. In other words, he is not shy in assuming as evident the worth of Freedom over the claims of Justice. Clearly, Freedom, not Justice, is his god-term.[19] His choice, which is not quite as self-evident as he might wish, is deeply related to his defense of the individual against the claims of the group. For Freedom is a value that attaches to the individual, whereas Justice is a value that involves social relations. And it is entirely possible—Plato saw its plausibility clearly—that a society should choose Justice as a prelude to Liberty and make the social bonds the necessary condition for individual freedom.

BOUNDED FREEDOM

Freedom is not something innate in humans. As Hannah Arendt noted, it is something we win or lose at the level of the social. Hence, before we can possess freedom, we must have rules that regulate our expectations and guide our choices. Such rules must be grounded on a conception of social bonds that can only be long lasting if Justice sustains it. The long tradition of conservative social thinkers—from Plato through Hegel, Durkheim, and Parsons—has made a good case for the social as a sine qua non of the individual. Karl Popper's—and Vargas Llosa's—dismissal of their contribution to our understanding of the human condition seems premature and misguided.

Sir Isaiah Berlin (1909–97) understood liberty as having two sides: its negative side has to do with the protection of individuals from oppression; its positive side has to do with individual agency. Over the years, Vargas Llosa has shown he has taken Berlin's entire effort quite seriously. But he is particularly interested in the positive aspects of liberty. He believes it makes possible creativity and hence progress. However, as we have seen, given his conservative position, the nagging question has been how to secure positive liberty without succumbing to nihilism. He solves the problem by relying on the Market. It is the Market that allows for creativity within certain self-given rules. If this is so, the Market expresses more than any other institution the desire for the reconciliation of Individual and Society.

NEOLIBERAL ECONOMICS

Surveying the political landscape of Latin America over the last few decades, Vargas Llosa sees that despite nagging setbacks, posed by the Cuban experiment on the one hand and right-wing would-be dictators on the other, political liberty has been largely achieved. At least on this score, Latin Americans are finally approximating the ways of the West. He also sees, however, that such political gains are precarious. They could easily be overturned by social movements, products of misguided resentment or impatience.[20] In other words, as in the rest of the Western world, in order to thrive, these ways of being necessitate a solid economic base.

DEPENDENCY THEORIES

Vargas Llosa sees several reasons for Latin America's economic backwardness. One of those reasons can be understood as a question of mentality, because, generally speaking, Latin Americans have traditionally tended to see their failures as the result of exogenous designs. They have seldom been willing to take a hard look into their own actions to redress their shortcomings. In the economic field, Vargas Llosa believes, this mentality had become very apparent by the middle of this century. Dependency Theory, the best-known school of economic thought produced by Latin Americans, cemented the myth that if the subcontinent found itself on the periphery of economic growth, it was because of foreign designs.[21]

What was most interesting, and showed the strength of the victim mentality most clearly, was the fact that the myth was not only perpetuated by a left-wing cultural elite; it was also embraced by members of the ruling classes. Protectionism, mercantilism, and neofeudalism just as much as radical populism are all dependent on such a myth in order to survive in the twentieth century. For the plain fact is, Vargas Llosa holds, that in today's international economic order, countries and continents can elect to be rich or poor.[22] In the new global economy, every population on earth can find profit by exploiting its comparative advantages. As it has happened with other convenient myths, Vargas Llosa claims, this one will also eventually be exploded by historical events.

THE *INFORMALES*

As early as the eighties, Vargas Llosa saw the Peruvian people standing ready to free themselves from the victim mentality. New entrepreneurs, from the wealthiest and the poorest sectors of Peru, were emerging. The myth of foreign designs, nurtured by complacent rentiers and imitative intellectuals, was being dismantled in the marketplace. In a magnificent return to his marxist days, Vargas Llosa invested a social group, the *informales*, with the messianic task of liberating all Latin Americans.[23] The *informales*, heroic entrepreneurs laboring at the edges of the top-heavy State, not the proletarians, are the true subject-objects of History. Like Marx before him, Vargas Llosa expected the proclaimed messianic group to heed the call.[24]

As it turned out, the *informales*—like the proletarians before them—were not eager to follow. They rebuked their self-proclaimed standard-bearer on at least one occasion: during Vargas Llosa's bid for the presidency of his old country. The reasons for their rebuke were complex. For one thing, the *informales* never really achieved the coherence of an independent class or interest group. For another, the meager but stable entitlements—in health, housing, and education— expected from the State made possible for many their entrance into the informal economy. Penny capitalism was never expected to sustain them fully. More generally, it appears penny capitalism thrives in the absence of regulation and disappears as it enters rule-bound market systems. Be that as it may, the fact remains that the identified class of new entrepreneurs did not opt for what seemed to Vargas Llosa the most reasonable and enlightened course of action.

THE INVISIBLE HAND

Vargas Llosa's neoliberal ideology harks back to an ancient belief; a belief that attained high currency during the European Enlightenment and gave much hope to philosophers like Kant and Hegel and economists like Adam Smith. At the core of that belief is the notion that unity can be born of difference, like peace out of conflict. To make the belief plausible, of course, these great men posited an invisible force hovering over and often goading the humans engaged in the pursuit of their own interests. This was the function Kant assigned to Nature,

Hegel to the cunning of Reason, and Smith to the Invisible Hand. In other words, it was not from ideological coherence or rational choice that unity and peace—with whatever modicum of happiness they might bring us—are to be attained, but from the multiplicity of self-grounded interests.[25]

The ancient belief was largely abandoned as a serious sociotheoretical position by the end of the nineteenth century. This was not surprising. At its core, it went against the overall ideals of the Enlightenment. Indeed, why would humans abandon the Reason-given idea of fashioning their Society in accordance with the demands of thought and leave it up to chance, luck, or coincidence, or perhaps worse, to the play of nonrational forces, to bring about the Good Society? Furthermore, given the Enlightenment's conception of human beings as potentially prudent free agents, was it not desirable that the process by which the Good Society is brought about should exhibit Freedom and Justice?

The philosophers of the Enlightenment—even Kant, for whom eudaemonism was anathema—believe God guaranteed that happiness would eventually be proportionate to virtue. In the context of the market, self-grounded desire, bounded by Christian virtue, would eventually produce the common good. As Weber noted, the Puritan toiled in his calling, certain that all individual action had a common purpose: God's glory. Within Calvinism, Weber's premier exemplar of the Protestant ethic, the Signification Corollary—psychologically necessary after Calvin's death—could only be taken as an indication of salvation if success was achieved according to rules and moral correctness. In short, the market became the field of action of individual effort because everyone assumed God guaranteed the final outcome.

DICTATORSHIP AND NEOLIBERALISM

As Weber was wont to wonder: why should this very peculiar understanding of humanity's relation to the Divine be taken as the ground for all our hopes? In effect, after the Enlightenment, as scoffers claimed God to be dead, the guarantee that individual actions would produce the common good was radically questioned. The marxist critique of the Market as dehumanizing was taken to heart even by theologians. And now, how do we ground this image of the production of the common good?

In a correct reading of history, and very much like the philosophers and economists of the Enlightenment, Vargas Llosa holds that for the Market to function well, rules must be respected.[26] But there is no articulation of the grounds for why this should be so. Often he talks as if, as in the case of religion, the ground is sheer utility. But, as we have seen, utility concerns do not solve Glaucon's challenge: why should anyone who does not fear being caught play by the rules? Vargas Llosa wants to distance himself from the authoritarian imposition of obedience to rules.[27] But it is not clear why one should avoid an equivalent of the Protestant fear of God's wrath as grounds for not transgressing rules. In other words, why shouldn't dictatorship be the backbone of the neoliberal utopia?

SURVIVAL OF THE FITTEST

It could be argued that entering the Market is a question of survival. Regardless of motives, the fact of the matter is that the capitalist system is already in place around the world, and to survive it is necessary to adapt. Old values must be given up and new ones appropriated from the already vast capitalist inventory. This view does not judge traditional cultures as morally inferior but as anachronistic with respect to survival. The request is that individuals learn to play a new game. And the best way to do that is by mimicking those who are already successful. If Catholic, learn to be Protestant; if peasant, learn how to be urban; if weak, how to be strong.

This necessary transvaluation of values, like life itself, is not without pain. Giving up dysfunctional values, Vargas Llosa accepts, following Milton Friedman, is as painful as it is for an addict to give up drugs. And there is no question that some will win and some will lose in the new world order. Some will end up dehumanized and exploited, but others will achieve the highest levels of humanity. In reality, claims Vargas Llosa, there is no other choice. To remain within the old system is even more painful and dehumanizing. Who would want anyone to live under the oppression of illiteracy, illness, and myth? Given the choice, individuals will rationally choose to enter the new game and take their chances. There is no need for authoritarian repression in order to play in the new order; only for opportunities to act according to self-interest.[28]

FALSE CONSCIOUSNESS

It was a sign of utter false consciousness, Vargas Llosa would eventually claim, that the Peruvian Many did not choose to follow him. Echoing Milton Friedman, he believed the drugs of entitlement and charity were too strong for them to choose freedom. The same could be said of the ruling classes.[29] They all let the opportunity to enter the game pass them by. In doing so, they buried their heads in the sand. The fact of the matter is, he would hold, that their world is of the past. They cannot hope to attain the highest levels of humanity by holding on to the crutches of anachronistic value systems.

7

✛

Writer and Politico

If the decadence, impoverishment, terrorism and constant crises had not made governing the country an almost impossible challenge, it would never have entered my head to take on the task.

—M. Vargas Llosa

AGONISTIC DAEMONS

In his essay on the religious rejections of the world, Max Weber identifies several modern daemons loose in the world making mischief. These daemons—aesthetics, politics, economics, science, the erotic—are fundamentally agonistic. Each attempts to seize the heart of disoriented individuals. In the end, offers Weber with sadness, in an increasingly disenchanted world, a world devoid of ultimate ends, modern individuals must choose one daemon and make the best of a dismal situation. Vargas Llosa's conception of the relationship between two fundamental daemons, aesthetics and politics, follows the outlines of Weber's insights.

In the beginning, Vargas Llosa tells us, he felt literature was more important than politics.[1] He stayed away from politics not because he had not yet felt the lure of power—he had already felt the seduction of power as a member of Cahuide, one of the many armchair marxist groups at San Marcos University—but so as to embrace his true vocation: literature. As he embraced his aesthetic daemon, he found it to be jealous and demanding. Against all odds, however, he heeded its demands and eventually was rewarded: he became a writer.

He managed to stay virtually out of party politics until the early 1980s. Then, he tells us, spurred into action by the unsavory deeds of a mystagogue, Alan García, ex-president of Peru, and with much trepidation, he drew closer to the world of power. His entrance into politics was not smooth. In large measure, this was because he was already a world-renowned writer in the Latin American tradition. That is, Vargas Llosa entered the fray feeling upon his shoulders the moral obligation peculiar to those whom Hegel called world-historical individuals: he entered politics offering salvation.

The agonistic nature of the modern daemons was clear to Vargas Llosa very early on. He realized that power strives to grow and to endure.[2] Those under its influence feel it as an obsession, a consuming, visceral need. The demands of the aesthetic daemon are equally compelling and utterly other: it flourishes by questioning the facticity of power.[3] As Weber had understood, two such antagonistic urges could not coexist for long in a human's heart, but neither could they abandon the struggle for supremacy.

POLITICAL DAEMON

Vargas Llosa eluded the subtle and constant lure of power for years. When the temptation was too strong, he looked into his heart and realized that, if he was to follow a new daemon at all, he had to do it with total conviction and determination. And he did. For a short while, he tells us, he became as monomaniacal in politics as he had been in literature. In the end, of course, he was forced to come to the conclusion that his role as world-historical individual was not to be fulfilled, at least not in the political arena. He then made a candid but cardinal error: he confessed he had never stopped being suspicious of all power, that he had never really abandoned his first daemon, that he was more than glad to return to his books. His critics sounded off: sour grapes.

The reaction of the author was not atypical, especially in Latin America. Intellectuals there have always positioned themselves as outsiders, as determined critics; but they have always been close to and tempted by power. Sometimes the lure of power has been irresistible. They have then joined the fray, only to be disappointed. Often, they have then forsaken their newly adopted daemon and gone back to their more natural pugilistic postures as outsiders. The particulars of Vargas Llosa's retreat were also not atypical. It often happens in Peruvian politics that self-appointed leaders are left behind by their would-be followers, as new leaders rise to announce a new beginning. Alberto Fujimori's appeal among significant sectors of entrepreneurs and *informales* is only one example.

THE WORLD-HISTORICAL INDIVIDUAL IS FORSAKEN

In 1990 Peruvians lost an occasion to help reenact the melodrama of the bid for power by a nineteenth-century world-historical individual: the brooding, honest, passionate man enters the fray—the business of barbarians, according to Napoleon—against his wishes and better judgment but for the sake of duty and "the people," only to suffer the unjust injuries inflicted by lesser souls. Of course, his class and culture—embodied by men like ex-presidents José Luís Bustamante y Rivero and Fernando Belaunde Terry—demanded the writer's sacrifice. But perhaps such enactments are no longer possible at the turn of the millennium; a time when the impertinent Many are turning politics into a mundane, murky, carnivalesque affair.

Max Weber noted that an individual has the calling for politics if he can reconcile in his heart the demands of the ethics of responsibility and the ethics of ultimate ends. The first requires that due weight be given to the mundane concerns of the Many; the latter, that one stand firm against such concerns for the sake of uncompromised and uncompromising values. Vargas Llosa believed he had heard the call to politics. But all too soon he learned he had no stomach for the daily life of fears, deceptions, intrigues, conspiracies, and betrayals. Despite, or because of, his aseptic approach to political campaigning, which he secured by surrounding himself with a coterie of postmodern advisors and their gadgets, he never got close to the Many. He never saw past their sweaty palms, their simulation, dissimulation, and sycophancy. He despised the whole affair.[4] He was left with firm convictions and uncompromising values. In the end, therefore, he had to concede he was not cut out for politics.[5]

THE ART OF COMPROMISE

During the elections of 1990, ex-president Belaunde Terry continued to act as if he lived in a country ruled by a small class in full possession of a strong neocolonial ideology. In such a scenario, political will and economic interest coincided, and ruling over the Many could be both wise and effective. Order and civility were secured through the teaching of good manners and an appeal to authority. Vargas Llosa shared only part of that vision. He has never been uncomfortable claiming membership in the upper classes; but he has also shown himself to be a child of the sixties who has often rebelled against ascribed privileges. By the late 1980s, however, the reasons for his rebellion, brewing since at least the late sixties, had changed dramatically. If before he attacked the neocolonial ideology from the left, he now attacked it from the right. Marxist-influenced economic analysis had given way to a neoliberal defense of the Market.

During his campaign, Vargas Llosa insisted—following an old Peruvian rhetorical device—that only the Market could save Peru. In his scenario, classes would dissolve in the icy waters of calculation, phenotypic characteristics would fall like a change of skin, and barbarians would learn to compete on the internet. As for the State, it resembled its nineteenth-century conception: a police force that secures order and protects contracts.

There were several problems with this scenario. First, in the 1990s it was impossible to deregulate and privatize the economy without great pain to the Many. Second, it was wishful thinking to believe Peruvians would want to revert to a nineteenth-century conception of the State and vote to dismantle the—however modest—welfare system that was in place. Third, to uphold the Market as the proper adjudicator of worth and success Vargas Llosa had to show he had not profited from his class and connections. An impossible task. And so, confronted by the mundane concerns of politics, attempting to reconcile the ethics of responsibility with the ethics of ultimate ends, he tried to learn the art of compromise.[6] He ended up welcoming into his camp the traditional politicos of his class.

SUSPICIONS

His upper-class origins were both a help and a liability during the campaign. On the one hand, he had learned to respect his servants and to see himself as a successor of a long line of public men.[7] This ingratiated him with the traditional, if shrinking, pockets of power. On the other hand, his animosity against the dictatorial populism of Manuel Apolinario Odría and Victor Raúl Haya de la Torre was visceral and bordered on the personal. (Odría had deposed Vargas Llosa's great-uncle, José Luís Bustamante y Rivero, and the Llosa clan has never forgotten that Victor Raúl Haya de la Torre had attacked the same patriarch in public.) Once made public, these animosities did not help Vargas Llosa's case among Haya de la Torre's followers in the north and among those around Lima who still remembered Odría's populist generosity.

Vargas Llosa failed to free himself from the strings of family and class. It ought not to have been surprising, therefore, that the Many were suspicious of his embrace of the Market from the beginning. They were aware that he and his family and class had profited, psychologically and materially, from traditional, unjust social structures. The writer/candidate was never able to convince the masses that he was different from any other member of his clan. In a candid self- and cultural critique, written shortly after his electoral defeat, Vargas Llosa acknowledged these entanglements. He then claimed that class resentment had been a significant factor in his defeat.[8] In a text in which resentment and insight are mingled, he charged that the Many had been incapable of seeing beyond their prejudices and had let a great opportunity pass them by.

THE MESSENGER MUST DIE

If one is willing to give the Peruvian Many the benefit of the doubt, of course, one could argue that Vargas Llosa's political defeat was in significant part a rebuke for practices the candidate had himself risen to eliminate: cronyism, nepotism, class privileges, unfair advantages in the marketplace. The Many, one could argue, had heard a message that required they do away with the messenger.

RACIAL POLITICS

According to Vargas Llosa, not only class but racial prejudices had been a factor. The exuberant support shown by well-to-do whites for his candidacy, he claimed, had awakened among the Many not only their envy but their (reverse) racism. Demagogues in the other camp only needed to exacerbate a racial hatred that had been kept just below the surface since before the conquest and that flares up from time to time with barbaric force, like the proverbial return of the repressed.[9] Alberto Fujimori and his coterie, *vivos* all, knew what they were doing when they appealed to the dark side of Peru.[10]

For better or for worse, though, Vargas Llosa and his supporters were also products of Peruvian culture. Consequently, his post facto insight ricochets in the enemy camp, escapes, and enters his own. It was clear to Peruvian voters that Vargas Llosa's supporters' racist attacks against Alberto Fujimori were vicious.[11] The writer/candidate tells us he was not happy with such abuses; but he was unwilling and/or unable to stop them. Even after the debacle, Vargas Llosa himself does not escape the prison house of clichés and prejudices. He tells us that he first knew of Alberto Fujimori as "a character as enigmatic as he was efficient, of whom I was never able to know much, only that he was a nisei and karate expert."[12]

KITCHEN CABINET

The writer/candidate was uncomfortable campaigning in a backward country like Peru.[13] Examining closely his complaints and overall political critique, it appears that he would have preferred to run for membership in the British Parliament. But, surely, it must not always have been like that. There was a time when he truly believed that, even in Peru, honest and well-articulated insights had a chance of winning in the marketplace of ideas. His bitterness and disappointment must have issued from his understanding that politics, especially in barbarous Peru, does not thrive on clarity and conviction but on the shadows of betrayals and deception.

Following Margaret Thatcher's advice, Vargas Llosa surrounded himself with people of similar ideas and background—mostly white and privileged.[14] A list of the names of the entrepreneurs who supported him gave the impression they were citizens of a different country. There was little room for *cholos* in his so-called Kitchen Cabinet.[15] He trusted the gurus of postmodern politics—Americans and Europeans—who in turn trusted their tools: exit polls, focus groups, media blitzes, simulated elections, and computers. Reading the descriptions of his headquarters in the Sheraton Hotel gives the impression he was running a very modern campaign—in a premodern country.

CULTURE AND POLITICS

Early in the campaign Vargas Llosa courted the international and Peruvian cultural elite. Since he was an international star (he had even appeared as a juror for a Miss Universe beauty pageant in Lima), it was not difficult to find artists and personalities—singers, beauty queens, television hosts—willing to share in the limelight. Also, following an old Peruvian tradition, perhaps an echo from Machiavelli's *Prince*, he showed himself to the people as someone they could look up to: benevolent but distant. He acted presidentially and moved on the campaign trail with an elegance that gave the impression he possessed great power and wealth.

Initially, these extraordinary accoutrements gained him popularity. He led all the polls by wide margins. But, in the end, his accoutrements did little to erase the image of the candidate as someone out of touch with the Peruvian people. In Peruvian politics, it seems, a leader may detest the ways of the Many, but unless he is able to understand such ways and work within them, he has little chance of leading the Many toward change.

SIMULACRE

Even an extraordinarily insulated candidate, however, cannot but feel when victory is escaping through his fingers. Vargas Llosa sensed his popularity in the polls was not a true measure of his political clout among the Many. He sensed it was superficial, a product of the electronic age, a simulacre. Seeing the campaign to save Peru in jeopardy, much against his taste Vargas Llosa harked back to tried and true *huachafo* tactics for winning elections. He pressed the flesh more eagerly; his wife and other good ladies from high society organized social teas and made excursions to poor neighborhoods to bring gifts and publicize the plight of the poor; incense was burned and processions organized.[16] These late efforts were not enough; perhaps they were never more than halfheartedly undertaken.

SOUR GRAPES

In defeat, Vargas Llosa appeared hurt and despondent. He concluded the barbarians had misunderstood his message in large part because they were duped by his enigmatic opponent. Less subtle minds and spirits in his camp were reduced to using obscene language to explain the electoral will of the Many. Sadly, it seemed that after the debacle Vargas Llosa and his closest followers reverted to old habits: to attacking as a *vivo*—hard and low.[17] A pity. There was no civic lesson learned. If the Many had declined his invitation to follow him up to the light, he had the obligation, as Socrates might have counseled, to go down to their cave, over and over again. For once the task has been seen clearly there can be no substitute for perseverance.

8

History and Freedom

When we were told that by freedom we understood free-enterprise, we did very little to dispel this monstrous falsehood. . . .

–H. Arendt

CONQUEST AND SALVATION

Most intellectuals who have espoused the values of the Enlightenment believe history moves unidirectionally. Some, like Hegel or Kant, held on to teleological hopes. Others, like Darwin or Marx, posited the existence of identifiable forces—born of nature and in time—that goad present action toward a discernible though only immediate future. In either case, the cardinal notion of Progress gave footing to hope and, hence, to willful European action. Without the notion of Progress, the deeds of European colonialism, so closely associated with the values of the Enlightenment, would have been deprived of their human face. For, in the unidirectional movement of history, the guilt that issued from inhuman deeds was assuaged with the belief in the inevitable advancement of humanity toward salvation.

THE GUIDING HAND

Following Karl Popper's attack on "historicist" philosophy, Vargas Llosa accuses Marx of having invented the iron laws of history.[1] History, he claims, contra Marx and echoing many, does not show an inner dialectic of succeeding stages leading up to a communist society; nor does it show class struggle as the key to understanding present chaos and future redemption.

But his attack on his old master is not as radical as it might appear. For Vargas Llosa does not wish to claim there are no discernible patterns in history. Nor does he wish to claim that the future is utterly open. On the contrary. He seems to reassert the Enlightenment's view that there is indeed discernible progress in history; that such progress shows a straining to unidirectionality; and that, against all warnings, there are indeed identifiable mechanisms propelling humans toward a better future.

What are, then, the forces prodding humans toward a better future? Hard to tell. On this matter, Vargas Llosa's social philosophy shows special kinship with that of Adam Smith. From his sociotheoretical works, one gets the impression he believes there is something not quite graspable by human consciousness yet palpably present in human affairs, which guides humanity out of chaos and toward lawful freedom. As in the case of the mischievous modern daemons, that "something" does not appear to be natural (biological) or spiritual in character. In fact, sometimes it seems as though it might be a human (historical) construct—but the construction has not been consciously done, at least not so far. As with such phenomena as electricity, we seem to know that "something" only through its effects: we know we are in the presence of a new, and hence superior, historical stage when *Individual Freedom* is enhanced.[2]

THE INDIVIDUAL AND SOCIETY

The Judeo-Christian tradition, particularly in Paul's foundational hermeneutic effort, nurtured individual freedom by placing the notion of a soul at the core of its teaching. But that tradition, with few possible exceptions, such as radical Calvinism, never conceived of the Individual as a good gained over against Community.[3] Minimally, the individual soul drew strength from communal ritual. The antinomy of the Individual and Society was solved with reference to an internally given Divine Love that made Communion possible.

With the hoped-for collapse of the Judeo-Christian tradition—wishful thinking of secular harbingers of modernity—modern social theorists believed the traditional solution to such a fundamental antinomy no longer worked. It had been the casualty of the incessant progress of humanity through time. There was, therefore, no way to repair it. Hence, theorists prepared themselves to shoulder the responsibility of giving a new solution to the antinomy of the Individual and Society. They relied on Reason. But these social theorists, from Marx to Pareto and from Freud to Mead, did not conceive of the Individual as a good gained over against Community either. In fact, all of the Enlightenment's solutions to the central antinomy of modern life made room for the integrative and life-enhancing embrace of community.

THE INDIVIDUAL AS A GOOD-IN-ITSELF

In the first instance, Vargas Llosa appears to follow the sociotheoretical tradition. He appears to accept that there is an inextricable relationship between Individual and Society; that individuality is gained in the interactive process taking place within social formations. But he goes beyond most modern social theorists to hold that, once the Individual emerged, both as a fact and as a value, in Western civilization, the safeguarding of his needs must, *prima facie*, override the interests of his community. In short, he goes on to view the Individual as a Good-in-Itself.

Given the long trajectory of the Western discourse on the antinomy of the Individual and Society, it seems such a claim stands in need of further substantiation. For the matter involves more than an understanding of the relative value of each term of the antinomy. It involves the thorny issues of incommensural values. And not even Freud, for whom civilization advances at the expense of the individual, believed the Individual could exist outside the life-regulating demands of civilization. Durkheim put it bluntly: not only the notion of an Individual but the value of such a notion is socially produced and sustained. In fact, for the sociotheoretical tradition as a whole, questions concerning the value of the individual always involve the values of a community. Unless one is prepared to adduce clearly mystical or theological grounds, the notion of the Individual-as-Such stands in need of defense.

OPTING FOR FREEDOM

Something similar can be said regarding the notion of Freedom. Few among moderns can honestly accept the old theological standpoint: humans are born free. Discussions on the ontological nature of human freedom seem echoes from a world largely bypassed by modern life. As Hannah Arendt masterfully sustained: individual freedom emerges in and through communal life; individual rights and liberties must always be understood as aspects of the body social. In short, there are no inalienable rights—except those that are socially produced. This view leaves open the possibility that, in given circumstances, the body social might trade in Individual Freedom for other foundational values.

The matter is fundamental. To paraphrase Nietzsche: what if the body social opts for Unfreedom? Or, to put it less stridently: why not celebrate Justice or Honor as the master category for our times? In a world supposedly devoid of theological residues, what sustains the preemptive claim of Individual Freedom over any other master category?

Here, too, Vargas Llosa follows the coattails of the Enlightenment and answers with an appeal to the notion of Progress: societies that have Honor, Justice, or other master categories—God, Race, Beauty—in the place of Individual Freedom are decidedly backward, surpassed. His is an utterly nonrelativist standpoint. The value of Individual Freedom, nurtured and developed by Western social practices, is presented as a Good-in-Itself.

FREEDOM AND BARBARISM

Vargas Llosa sees the Inca empire as part of a barbarous time now thankfully receding into the past. The absence of Individual Freedom, as its master category, indicates the full extent of its backwardness. Very much like Inca Garcilaso de la Vega, Vargas Llosa understands the encounter between the Inca empire and the Europeans as a perhaps regrettable but inevitable progression of humanity. Unlike writers like José María Arguedas, he views the pre-Columbian past as something Peruvians are in desperate need of leaving behind. Knowledge of that past cannot be achieved for the sake of self-knowledge or cultural reconciliation; it is necessary to tame its evil influences.[4]

RESENTMENT

Inca Garcilaso de la Vega, one of the better-educated Peruvians of his time, left Peru, the land of his mother, for Spain, the land of his father. The retracing of his father's steps must have been life affirming. The approach to the dreamed home of civilizers must have been at once humbling and exhilarating. And yet, in the dark hours of his self-imposed exile, the Peruvian writer must have felt Mother Spain a mysterious, alien world. Perhaps it was to work through a loneliness brought about by the sounds and smells of strange shores that the mestizo man invented the temporal and spatial contours of his forsaken native land. Perhaps the hue of nostalgia in *Los comentarios reales* reflects feelings of dreaded temporal and spatial distances. Perhaps in those pages remembrance is truly Desire satisfied.

The retracing of the ancestor's footsteps has also led Vargas Llosa back to Spain. But unlike Inca Garcilaso de la Vega, it seems he has no need to work through loneliness. Perhaps this is because time and space have been nearly tamed by the forces of modernity. In any case, there is no hue of nostalgia in his books. Rather, the polycephalous, dismal problems of Peru are so intrusive, they leave room only for shame. As a self-defined white European urban man, he quiets such feelings by praising those aspects of Peru that could make possible its insertion in the European tradition while proclaiming his distance from everything smacking of the non-Western and barbaric. The feelings of shame crowd out any nostalgia for a mestizo land, a mestizo history, mestizo dreams. As with the narrator of *El hablador*, mestizo Peru intrudes into his European reveries as an unwelcome ghost. He understands that mestizo apparition—a rotten carcass, the color of excrement—is the necessary magma for his creative impulse.[5] But he also understands it as a reminder of the distance between his claim to the European tradition of his ancestors and the reality of his past, of his Peruvian past, which constitutes a part of his being. Perhaps that is why, if Inca Garcilaso de la Vega wrote with nostalgia, Vargas Llosa writes with resentment.

THE SOCIALIST NEW MAN

In the 1920s José Carlos Mariátegui argued that only socialism could save Peru from its poverty and oppression. After that, socialist thought, particularly in its marxist animus, became part of the conversation concerning the future of Peru. Those who lived in the country during the middle decades of this century could not but participate in such a conversation. Vargas Llosa was no exception. He, too, believed in socialism then, even if only from a literary perspective. With other comrades, he expected the triumph of the revolution criss-crossing the Latin American landscape like a firebrand. He, too, hoped for the inception of a Socialist Society for a New Man. But, he tells us, hard experience disabused him of such naive beliefs. In time, he came to understand that the drive to political victory bore ill will against those called by the aesthetic daemon. It was inevitable: by the eighties he and his old comrades had become declared enemies.

AN OLD MAN

The socialist image of a New Society for a New Man was already old. Simon Bolivar had sketched its dimensions a century before. In fact, socialists well knew they were drawing strength from a long-cherished Dream of the Latin American cultural elites: the foundation of a Latin American Nation for a New Man. So, when Vargas Llosa abandoned socialism, he had no problem retaining the cherished dream at the core of his sociopolitical thought. This helps to explain his disdain for all types of nationalism. In fact, Vargas Llosa wishes to distinguish between patriotism and nationalism. A patriot's feelings for his country, he argues, ought to be, like his religion, a private affair. When it becomes public, it is easily conflated with nationalism. And nationalism quickly turns into protectionism, isolationism, and chauvinism. In short, nationalism is an impediment to the realization of the Dream of a Latin American Nation.[6]

SUBLATIONS

As might be expected, the realization of the cherished Dream presupposes the sublation of cultural pluralism across Latin America. There have been two versions of such sublation. For thinkers like Bolivar, Vasconcelos, Haya de la Torre, and Mariátegui, the overcoming of cultural pluralism has meant the ideological embrace of the mestizo as the New Man. For others, such as José Enrique Rodó, Antonio Caso, and Faustino Sarmiento, the realization of the Nation would be possible if and only if it is squarely based on the European culture.

As might be expected, Vargas Llosa stands closer to the latter group of intellectuals. For him, the only way to realize the Dream is to embrace, fully, European values. All other positions are either unrealistic or ideological. In his vision of the future, the history of the non-European peoples in Latin America must be approached with exorcist intentions.

CUBA

In Latin America, to be for or against socialism has always meant to be for or against the Cuban experiment. In the sixties, Vargas Llosa tells us, taking a stance for or against Cuba was akin to making a religious choice.[7] It is not surprising, therefore, that those who embraced the Cuban revolution in the sixties and repudiated it a decade or two later seem to have gone through some sort of religious conversion. The phenomena is typical not only of Latin America, of course. It is repeated all over the world in nuanced ways. At its extremes, the resolution of such experiences involves a heartfelt repentance of old choices and an eager espousal of their antipodes: fascism or neoliberalism. As in most existential choices, the clearer the chosen alternative the cleaner the resolution.

As is common in religious conversions, believers in new political ideologies feel compelled to explain to themselves and their new comrades the choices made in their pasts. Some come to see past choices and experiences as offering intimations of the truth finally found. Such revision of biography does not always involve a radical repudiation of the past. Others, however, come to see past choices and experiences as aspects of a nightmare from which they are glad to have finally awakened. In this case, the past is often renounced. It is in this latter sense that Vargas Llosa now sees his past choices and allegiances. He finds nothing true or good in his and his comrades' youthful stances. At best, he explains the martyrdom of socialists across the Nation as the misguided action of well-intentioned fanatics.[8]

WHERE ALL THE BONES ARE BURIED

There is nothing worse—or better—than a new convert to an ideology; for he knows where all the bones are buried. Looking back, revising the collective past, the newly virtuous man can confront old comrades with all-too-human, uncomfortable facts. And Vargas Llosa is quite thorough in his Truthtelling effort: for the most part, left-wing intellectuals are all *vivos*, simulators and dissimulators, professional radicals, eager to accept the bribes of scholarships, travels, stipends, etc., from the capitalist centers of power they spend their lives denouncing.[9] They claim the high moral ground based on self-deception and outright lies. Among writers, Vargas Llosa cries, the better ones develop a split personality: as artists they are innovators; as cultural leaders they are subservient and/or simulators. To defend their wrong-headed choices, to keep their masks in place, the old comrades attack as *vivos*: low and hard. Most times, Vargas Llosa complains, this animus translates into a demonization of their critics.[10]

Vargas Llosa appears outraged at the fact that sophisticated capitalist states and corporations are shamelessly duped by cagey third-world intellectuals. But perhaps both the would-be duped and the cagey are *vivos* playing to win. The ones adversely affected by their antics are the *tontos* not willing or able to play the game. Vargas Llosa has always played to win.

LEFT-WING INTELLECTUALS

If Vargas Llosa's critique of Latin American intellectuals is quite determined, his attack on the left-wing Peruvian intellectual establishment is also visceral. He does not let any opportunity pass to vent his anger against an establishment that in his estimation smothers creative souls and cuts all rebels down to size.[11] As might be expected, in this critique, biographical and historical revisions coincide.

Before and during the dismal years of dictatorship, from Odría to Velasco Alvarado, offers Vargas Llosa, Peruvian intellectuals such as Porras Barrenechea, Jorge Basadre, Mariano Ibérico, and Honorio Delgado upheld the highest standards of Peruvian intellectual life. These old patricians taught the young generation—Vargas Llosa among them—the love of learning and dedication to hard work. By the sixties, as Peruvian society changed and newcomers, mostly lower-class mestizos, entered the hallowed grounds of universities and literary institutions, the old patrician leadership gave way to a polycephalous mass of simulators and dissimulators.[12]

This reading of Peruvian intellectual history is nostalgic and therefore somewhat misleading. As Gonzales Prada and Salazar Bondy made plain, there has never been a patrician leadership in Peru. If it existed at all, such leadership was available only to a small group within the small elite of would-be Europeans. In fact, the strengths and shortcomings of the new generation of Peruvian intellectuals might have much to do with the resistance they encountered in the old, incestuous establishment. Their distaste for the leadership of old patricians—and their contemporary admirers—might be the result of such experiences. The past always weighs heavily on the minds of the living.

9

Memory

The children, seated in a circle around the poet, will ask: "And all this you saw? You heard?"

"Yes."

"You were here?" the children will ask.

"No. None of our people who were here survived."

The poet will point to the moving clouds and the sway of the treetops.

"See the lances?" he will ask. "See the horses' hooves? The rain of arrows? The smoke? Listen," he will say, and put his ear against the ground, filled with explosions.

And he will teach them to smell history in the wind, to touch it in stones polished by the river, and to recognize its taste by chewing certain herbs, without hurry, as one chews on sadness.

—Quetzaltenango, 1524

THE PAST

The past is a communal experience. It is constantly receding from the collective memory, to which it owes its existence. As it recedes, the past inevitably changes. Inscription translates the collective desire to give permanence to what is always fleeting and no longer present. In some cultures and over time, inscription has tended to overshadow the collective will to remember.

In the West, and over millennia, the scribe worked ever more alone; his individual memory and vision stained the collective record. After him, the long and arduous search for objectivity—recording without judging—has culminated in today's reliance on machines to record events *sine ira et studio*. As a consequence, the past is less and less present in our souls. For only the art of history, not its science, can breathe life into past deeds. It is no wonder that postmodern man, tired of the effort entailed in withholding judgment, is more than willing to replace the search for objective Truth with a celebration of ever-changing individual and collective mythology.

GIFTED INDIVIDUALS

Individuals living in oral cultures are closer to their past, which does not mean they understand or control it. The past, still present within them, holds the fibers of their hearts and thus projects itself into the future. Inscription, if it exists, is a mnemonic device, a gift from the gods. But to keep the past present thusly has a high price; it must be constantly and earnestly re-invented. In such cases, the past is truly what the collective will and memory make of it. It is fragile. To the collective will, memory shows little room for dead facts. Whatever is to be retained for posterity is filtered by and woven into the tapestry of deeply felt values, desires, and dreams.

Despite the communal bonds that sustain desires and dreams, not even the most "primitive" culture can dispense with the solitary labor of a few gifted individuals who give preliminary form to what is to be kept from oblivion. In their form-giving intent, these gifted individuals, the Storytellers, begin the process of fashioning a world. This is one of the interesting insights to be gathered from Vargas Llosa's lifetime effort. He articulates it most fully in his novel *El hablador,* where "the one-who-speaks" is portrayed as both a vessel for and a forger of a past tending to a desired future.[1] In that image of *el hablador*, Vargas Llosa approximates Walter Benjamin's discussion of the Storyteller as forger and bearer of counsel.

THE STORYTELLER

In his marvelous evocation of Nikolai Leskov, Walter Benjamin tells us that, as far as the West is concerned, the Storyteller is a character now only dimly present in our collective memory. He no longer speaks; he is only spoken about. The Storyteller accompanied Western peoples on their trek past the pastoral epoch and up to the embryonic development of urban life, where he survived for some time among the shadows, beyond the lights. With the invention of the inscriptive machine, his role as mouthpiece for the gods and experience finally disappeared.

Vargas Llosa partially agrees. Only among such peoples as the Tasurinchi, living in the dark jungles of Peru, is *el hablador* still possible. The encounter of such primitive cultures with the West is therefore fateful. During and after the trauma of mutual recognition, the new Peruvians—the mestizos—learn to see the past as it is preserved through inscription.[2] They enter the city and hear the words of the Storytellers as if in a dream. But, at the same time, Vargas Llosa harbors the hope (or is it the ambition?) that the Storyteller of old has merely metamorphosed into the writer/critic of today.

THE NEW STORYTELLER

Like most writer/critics, Vargas Llosa is suspicious of Truth-seeking social scientists—inscriptors all; especially when they are on the goverment's payroll. In the case of Latin America, where rational discourse, Western and Puritan, has been only halfheartedly embraced, objectivity can be twisted by desire and bought for a price. Under such circumstances, and given the task of the writer/critic as discloser of Truth, Vargas Llosa believes, the writer has become a modern Storyteller.

The writer/critic shoulders the responsibility of recording the enduring experiences of a people. This means the record cannot be a litany of dead facts. The writer/critic lets the underlying Truth of his time speak through an art guided by individual and collective daemons. As in the pyschoanalytic session, the writer/Storyteller lets his unconscious reach out to the collective dreams and desires that surround him.

Echoing Max Weber, Vargas Llosa also holds that there can never be an objective account of past events. The official past, that is the past as recorded and disseminated through institutions such as schools and universities, for example, is always one-sided, cut to order by ever-changing desires and interests. More generally, and striking a postmodernist posture, Vargas Llosa holds that memory, collective as well as personal, is always tendentious. These truisms, he holds, are most evident in underdeveloped countries like Peru.[3] To be true to his calling, the Peruvian writer must constantly question and amend the official history—for the sake of Truth.

GRAVE DIGGERS

The corrective deed is not accomplished by rendering a "realist" account of events, however. A literary effort that does not reach beyond the ready-at-hand, to such things as individual and collective dreams and desires, will never be real enough. This has been, Vargas Llosa writes, the cardinal error of much "realist" fiction in Latin America. More often than not, such works resemble the accounts of the social sciences: the cataloguing of minutia, from unjust to heroic acts. Fiction must be free to disclose Truth in its own way. The writer must conceive of himself as, at once, rescuer and grave digger of the past. For the writer is like a vulture, nourished by "the putrid flesh of history."[4] There is no room for a pristine preservation of individual and collective deeds.

There is a strong "realist" dimension in Vargas Llosa's novels, of course. He borrows freely not only from biography—his own and those of people close to him—but also from the collective experiences of his time. In this narrow sense, he can be said to have contributed to saving certain events for posterity.[5] But his amending animus is not exhausted by the inscription of such resonant or obscure real events. The animus is more salient in his disclosure, through aesthetically accomplished fiction, of what lies around and underneath the minutia of data and dates. The Truth of literature endures, he offers, because it emerges from the very essence of the times; because it preserves the intentionally and unintentionally forgotten; because, through its intimating qualities, it makes present the ineffable. As we have seen, Vargas Llosa does not shrink from embracing the awesome responsibilities of the would-be Kantian genius.[6]

DISCLOSING TRUTH

In his essay on translation, Benjamin makes the following point: If there is something essential in human existence and longing, it must find expression in a pure language. No single language is therefore adequate to give presence to such essence. Each language touches on the Truth much as a tangent touches a circle. The task of the translator is to let the essential sediment inherent in one language spill over onto another, his own. Only by the accumulation of insights from different traditions might Truth be accessible for us humans.

In a similar though perhaps less sublime vein, we could say that there is a substratum of historical Truth that art discloses, that each artistic offering contributes to our understanding of or our approximation to such Truth. In this case, any account of the past could be, in principle, judged against that which was and which remains potentially accessible to us. Truth attaches to essences and hence it is distinguishable from error. Art would then be conceived as a privileged way of knowing; but not, necessarily, as a privileged medium in the process of creation. Much of the hermeneutic effort of the West over the last two millennia has rested on this epistemic conception of art.

THE AMENDING ANIMUS

On the other hand, it could be argued that there is no such thing as historical Truth; that the past is an all-too-human construction of real or imagined but always disputable events. If this is the case, then, literature cannot but exhibit an amending animus as it offers its Truth. If this is so, it must be accepted that such an animus is, in principle, sustainable by different writer/Storytellers expressing different politico-cultural tendencies. Aesthetic truths would manifest themselves in a multiplicity of even contradictory ways. The kinds of amendments made to an official history, for example, would depend, to significant degrees, on the particular cultural-political tendencies through which any given writer helps to construct and reconstruct the past.

In this case, the contribution of a gifted writer would lie, not so much in his ability to rescue what was, but in doing so in such a way that he adds something—depth, clarity, content—to that past. In other words, the amending animus of literature would have a formative dimension. Vargas Llosa's notion of the *elemento añadido* in great works of fiction dovetails nicely with these considerations. The past is understood as something constructed and not merely disclosed. In this sense, the writer/critic approximates the image of the Storyteller as inventor of the past.

AMBIVALENCES

Vargas Llosa's position regarding these two different conceptions of art is ambivalent. He mostly strikes a postmodernist posture and acknowledges the desirability of having all ideas regarding anything, including the past, play out publicly, in free exchange. Knowledge of the past is then seen as a communal undertaking. In that context, art is conceived as only one more factor in our collective construction of our past. At the same time, however, given the perils of holding an utterly relativist position, he often proffers his own ideas, as a writer/critic, as having some kind of preemptive status. He claims to offer Truth against the conscious or unconscious deception of others. In such cases, art is seen as a privileged way of knowing and the writer as someone-who-knows.

LITERATURE AND RECOGNITION

Fiction writing, argues Vargas Llosa, is in large measure an act of self-recognition and self-explanation. It is, preeminently, an encounter with the past. Through the inscriptive act, biography is brought up for inspection. Sometimes the inspection is carried out unwittingly; sometimes it is done in full awareness of the desire to dispel obscurities and to know. In the case of gifted writers, the effort toward self-recognition spills over onto a recognition of the psychohistorical traumas and resonances of an epoch. Vargas Llosa intends to exemplify these views in most of his fiction and in his critical works on such disparate writers as Flaubert, García Márquez, and José María Arguedas. In these works, biography is always connected to history by visible threads of meaning.

When successful, the connection is both enriching and treacherous. Enriching because through the prism of a gifted mind and soul the rest of us mortals gain a modicum of self-understanding and, perhaps, if we are realist enough, a measure of self-love. Treacherous because, desperate still to believe, we might take the experiences of the gifted soul as privileged windows into phantom essences. For biographies, even those of self-conscious writers, can only offer one-sided glimpses into our past. When used in art, biographies offer resonances, intimations, never certainty or ideas based on what philosophers would call a correspondence theory of truth.

RECONSTRUCTION IN FICTION

Within fictive reality, if there is no objective truth and humans are constantly reconstructing their past, then, Vargas Llosa reminds us, not only the narrator's point of view but the biographical and historical data offered as interpretive guideposts for the individual or collective past ought never to be taken at face value. In this sense, fictive reality presumably mirrors the real reality: it is utterly open-ended. The reader of fiction must himself construct and reconstruct truth in the world he chooses to enter. In other words, the omniscient narrator, like the social forces that gave him ground, is a thing of the past. The modern writer is a God-slayer and cannot offer a rounded Individual or Society without losing his realist vision. This is in large part why, for Vargas Llosa, the presentation of the different voices making up a fictive world is a central aim of the Total Novel.

RECONSTRUCTION THROUGH FICTION

As for the uses of biography in fiction for the reconstruction of our collective past, Vargas Llosa warns that literary points of view and their supporting data ought never to be taken as more than constructions and reconstructions done, at best knowingly, for the sake of the Good Lie. A narrator's account of how the world was during his high-school and university years, his tumultuous love affairs with kin and others, his relationship with parents, and so on, must all be taken for what they are: fictive accounts arranged in such a way as to produce an aesthetic effect.[7] Since it is impossible for humans to achieve an objective point of view, the writer's memory, as it gets translated into fiction, must always be suspect. Readers wishing to use fiction as a window to history must exercise radical suspicion. If, in the hands of a gifted writer, biography resonates with historical Truth, it cannot thereby claim a preemptive privilege. Aesthetics as a way of knowing is only one element in the social construction of the past.

RADICAL SUSPICION

The presentation of particular sociohistorical events through fiction, warns Vargas Llosa, must also be approached with suspicion. The aesthetical accomplishment of a novel lies not in the accuracy of presentation of historical detail but in its evocative force, in its making present the outlines and reso-nances of past clusters of events and meanings. Such evocative force is more often than not attained through a creative distortion of past events. The uses of the content of fiction as grounds for sociocultural reflection are therefore quite limited.

In novels like *La ciudad y los perros* and *Conversación en La Catedral*, both set in Peru's immediate past, Vargas Llosa goes a long way to redeem the prom-ise he sees in fiction. The provincial and yet complex Peruvian world of the fifties and sixties comes alive in these works. The lives and tribulations of main and secondary characters have a hue of familiarity about them, especially to those who lived through such difficult times. In fact, the evocative dimension of these novels is so superb it tempts us to forget that the world we are experienc-ing or re-experiencing as we read is the subjective offering of an author with his own daemons to pacify.

FICTIVE WORLDS

If we are to follow Vargas Llosa further still, we must admit that the lessons for the future—our present—drawn from such visions of the past must also be approached with radical suspicion. The pessimism that suffuses these two novels, for example, and lingers on as an unpleasant aftertaste, must be understood only as a plausible reading of a fictive past and its impingement on a fictive present. The fictive world offers no more than fictive musings. There are no lessons to be drawn, except perhaps for the characters that remain within the turned pages.

But, as we have already noted, the aesthetic-evocative force of accom-plished works of art prevents such easy circumscription. In works like *La cuidad y los perros* and *Conversacíon en La Catedral*, the fictive lessons and standpoints offered cannot but spill over into the nonfictive real conversation concerning the past and the future of Peru. In this sense, as an intricate part of the present conversation regarding the past and future of society, the aesthetic always turns political. Art cannot but contribute to self- and cultural under-standing, even if it can only do so as an utterly subjective offering. A writer/Storyteller's vision, though one among many, always strives to serve as an asymptote for action—even when he does not enter the political fray directly as Vargas Llosa did.

CONFESSIONS

The issues appear even more complicated when biographical and historical accounts are offered in the same literary but not explicitly fictive work. The temptation to use biography to organize and explain historical events and history to explain biographical experiences appears overwhelming. In extreme cases, the writer/Storyteller might be tempted to explain confessed biographical shortcomings by recourse to adduced adverse social circumstances.

Some of this can be appreciated in Vargas Llosa's *El pez en el agua*. The alternating stories in that work weave an account where the author's political failure is largely explained by the historical and contemporary shortcomings of the Peruvian people. In this work, fiction, history, and biography become a formidable weapon of attack and defense in contemporary debates regarding the past, present, and future of Peru. The tender confessions of childhood traumas in *El pez en el agua* do not blunt the tendency to make the personal political.

COMPETITION AND TRUTH

By making the personal political, the doors are open for political debates to be reduced to the hurling of insults, pouting, and back turning. The past (biographical or collective) is then no longer a source of insights, fictive or otherwise, much less a depository of partial truths tending to the construction of some historical Truth. Rather, it becomes an arsenal of possible weapons for, at best, winning arguments, at worst, revenge. It cannot be otherwise. For there will always be some among us who recall a different past and hence see a different future.

To be sure, in accordance with his overall theories, Vargas Llosa could hold that the marketplace of ideas remains as the only adjudicatory force between such competing claims. In the case of the offerings of fiction, the best story wins. And the best story is the one that tells the best lie. In such a competition, gifted writers would have the upper hand. In the case of memoirs, like *El pez en el agua*, for example, it might be the presentation of data and insight that gives them compelling force.

In either case, there is an implicit acknowledgment that truth, collective or otherwise, is always up for grabs. Furthermore, the construction and reconstruction of the past is not seen as a communal and cooperative process, an accumulation of dovetailing insights. Rather, Vargas Llosa adheres to the peculiar Enlightenment view (embraced by thinkers from Kant to Smith to Marx and with zeal more recently by Karl Popper) that Truth emerges, if at all, out of the competition of ideas; as peace emerges out of conflict.

Perhaps it is this agonistic conception of truth, be it in the construction of the past or of the future, that necessitates a determined defense of one's Truths. Not to fight fiercely for one's Truth might be construed as a relinquishing of responsibilities, especially if one believes oneself to be under the spell of daemons or touched by genius. The ambivalences in Vargas Llosa's theoretical stances would appear to be thusly reconciled.

10

✛

The Storyteller

The Story-teller is the figure in which the righteous man encounters himself.

—W. Benjamin

TRAUMAS OF CHILDHOOD

Despite nuanced and recurring distancing acts, Vargas Llosa must ultimately admit that he bears the scars of a man born in midcentury Peru. Because of his especially sensitive nature—which would serve him well as he matured into the leading intellectual of his generation—it was inevitable that such scars would include the childhood traumas perforce associated with insidious and invidious distinctions traced along class, race, and gender lines.

He was born into a situation in which his father, a man whose family had lost social standing to the point where he was considered a lower class *cholo*, was despised by the aristocratic Llosa family.[1] In the bosom of the Llosa tribe, as he is fond of calling his mother's extended family, young Mario learned to dislike his father and all that he represented—lower-class culture, violence, disregard for other people's feelings. As time passed, Vargas Llosa tells us, his father's words and deeds lent credence to the Llosas' damning appraisal of Mr. Vargas. Perhaps understandably, after halfhearted efforts at solidarity with his father's class, Vargas Llosa embraced the class and culture of his mother.

For long periods, mostly under the tutelage of his father, young Mario experienced life in Peru as a member of a struggling middle class. Upon his return from

Bolivia, where his grandfather had been sent as consul of Peru, he lived in Piura, a provincial town. He attended high school there, far away from the proper institutions of an upper-class upbringing. When he went back to Lima, he attended a parochial school in Magdalena del Mar, a middle-class neighborhood. In 1950, he entered the Colegio Militar Leoncio Prado, a mestizo institution. Even his life in Miraflores, then the residence of the cultured classes of Peru, was far from comfortable. In fact, perhaps more than at any other time in his life, in Miraflores he must have felt the pain of what sociologists call relative deprivation—and the visceral desire to belong.

A FLEETING NOSTALGIA

In his important essay on José María Arguedas, Vargas Llosa notes, with much feeling, how childhood traumas followed that truncated author and influenced the very core of his literature. He shows how the Andes, or rather their utopic construction, helped Arguedas fend off the daemons that caused him so much pain and that eventually asked for the ultimate sacrifice. In his reading, literature was for José María Arguedas at once a rebellious act and a crutch, a way of appeasing the daemons that inhabited his conflicted heart.

We know little of how young Mario was treated by the class-conscious scions of the Peruvian upper class. His long-standing sensitivity to be properly addressed—as Mr. Vargas Llosa and not simply as Mr. Vargas, as most Peruvians might—is surely in large measure due to his love for the family that nurtured him into adulthood. But, at least in part, it also reflects a sense of insecurity; an ill-concealed desire to claim definitive membership in the upper class.[2] In fact, his self-declared inclusion among the upper class, often subtle but quite unremitting, is offered in his writings with such seriousness that it does not permit self-irony. As one reads his works, there is never a doubt that between Mr. Mario Vargas Llosa and the Many there exists a veritable gap; a gap that existed, in the beginning, as that between a *niño bien* and the *huachafos*.[3]

It is a truism that not even the privileges of class and race can totally fend off the cruelties humans experience as they grow up. Vargas Llosa tells us, for example, that as a child he was sexually abused by a priest, and that he was subject to recurrent fears of physical and emotional abuse by his father.[4] To cope with these traumas he managed to cling to the world of his mother—to Miraflores, as an oasis, a quasi-mythical place to which he would always wish to return[5]—and to immerse himself in literature.[6] From the beginning, then, as for José María Arguedas, literature for Vargas Llosa was not only an act of rebellion against his father and what he represented, but also a crutch, a vehicle for carrying on his revenge against a world in need of re-inventing.[7]

MACHISMO AND REVOLUTION

As an adolescent, Vargas Llosa suffered the dictatorship of General Manuel A. Odría, the man who deposed José Luis Bustamante y Rivero, a cousin of Vargas Llosa's maternal grandfather.[8] Young Mario learned then to detest strong men in politics, just as he had learned to detest his father and what his father represented. His love for literature, which he understood as a rebellious act but which was seen by his father as a disturbing sign of an "effeminate nature," helped to land him as an intern in the Escuela Militar Leoncio Prado. In typical authoritarian fashion, it seems, Mr. Vargas was determined to "make a man" of young Mario. Vargas Llosa's visceral and public attack on Peruvian *machismo* appears to have its roots in this period of his life. Perhaps it was fitting that literature provided a safe haven for young Mario during the dismal two years he spent in the military school.

In 1953 Vargas Llosa entered San Marcos University in Lima. His decision to study at a state university was not welcomed by his mother's family, who would have preferred he attend the Pontificia Universidad Católica del Perú. At San Marcos he studied law and literature. He also joined Cahuide, a leftist political group. We might assume that he and his comrades met to discuss their support for workers, painted revolutionary slogans, and joined demonstrations. His early left-leaning socialistic idealism had its roots in those university years. Like other privileged intellectuals, young Mario advocated a revolution to do away with class privileges.[9]

THE ETHICS OF STORYTELLING

Well before he had read Flaubert on the nature of the creative act, Vargas Llosa felt tempted to use all his personal experiences as grist for his literary production.[10] When he finally read Flaubert, he was convinced that the use of biographical data was more than justified by his art; it was utterly indispensable. More still: he became convinced that the use of biographical data from other people was also justified and indispensable.[11] The defense of this pillage of the world has been presented by Vargas Llosa in different forms but it is centrally based on a nineteenth-century conception of genius. When he found that people were offended by the pillage, his defense was predictable: there is a clear difference between author and narrator;[12] even when a novel is based on biography or history, it never ceases to be fiction. The novel form, its aesthetic appeal, is seen as sufficient justification.

These considerations go to the very core of Vargas Llosa's conception of the ethic of a Storyteller. In that ethic, the comfort of real persons can be sacrificed for the sake of a larger, social or literary Truth. In his own case, the ethic is most clearly exemplified in his dealings with his Aunt Julia. There, private dreams, romantic confessions, and mundane shortcomings are manipulated for the sake of literature. Readers turn voyeurs. Of course, it is quite impossible to determine the truth content of such a relationship from the outside. Still, from the standpoint of the mores of his father, of his mother's family, of Peruvian society at large, and particularly of his aunt, the public airing of private affairs must have been experienced at least as embarrassing and highly unconventional.[13]

A HEALTHY EGO

The idea that self-importance goes hand-in-hand with self-sacrifice must have been instilled in young Mario by his mother's family. After all, he tells us, he was always thought of as "the hope of the family," the one designated to continue the long tradition established by the patricians in his tribe, a tribe that had always been involved in politics and for whom the possibility of being president of the cursed country had over the years become less attractive than making money. Within the Llosa tribe, becoming president was conceived not so much as the culmination of a personal ambition as the performance of a duty. To prepare young Mario to fulfill his destiny, his tribe had to develop in him a healthy ego, and perhaps a high degree of narcissism.[14] In time, as he came to believe himself a god with regard to his fictive worlds, it was easier to conceive of himself as one called to accomplish great things in the political arena as well. The deicidal act escaped the bounds of a book.

A DESIRE TO BELONG

These publicly discussed desires might only be part of the story, of course. Given young Mario's precarious social standing at the fringes of the upper classes from the beginning—which had forced him to invent the Miraflores utopia—it could be that he was urged to action by the unconscious desire to belong, properly, in his mother's world. Perhaps his well-deserved place in world literature would never have been enough. Perhaps his inclusion had to be felt and lived in the same circles that had looked at him askance when he was unknown. It is ironic that many among the upper class of Peru abandoned their love for Vargas Llosa, their world-historical candidate, soon after his defeat. Their reluctant love affair was followed by a series of recriminations in which insults were traded and old wounds reopened.

THE QUIXOTIC QUEST

In the late eighties, armed with the conviction of the strength of his vision—and perhaps urged by blind, ancient forces deposited by childhood traumas—Vargas

Llosa set out into the Peruvian political world in the quixotic quest to straighten what needed straightening. Since, willing himself to succeed, he had become a supplanter of God in fiction—despite the high hurdles that a country like Peru, barbaric and sad, had put in his path; since he had willed himself into an international citizen by jumping the fences of barbarism, he believed he could help others, less fortunate or less gifted, to achieve their potential and do something similar for themselves.[15]

To this end, as he had learned to do in literature, Vargas Llosa was willing to borrow the necessary weapons from the local and international culture—freely. If first he had armed himself with the rhetoric of Marxism, he now found in neoliberalism the ideology best suited for the daily deicidal act to be carried out by all Peruvians. Marx was exchanged for Popper as Sartre was for Camus. But the exchange did not erase all earlier valuations and hopes. For, much as Marx had done in the nineteenth century, Vargas Llosa rose ready to bid all Peruvians, as authors of their own fate, to reinvent their world and themselves in the process.

Unlike Freud, who coyly claimed not to have the courage to rise before humanity as a prophet, Vargas Llosa did not find daunting the prospect of presenting himself as a messianic figure. On the contrary, his Will to Truth and Will to Power found there a worthy field of resistance. As he had done in the quixotic quest to produce the Good Lie while standing in a cursed land, he now saw himself as a world-historical politico, ready to tackle a new goal against impossible odds. Indeed, "if the decadence, impoverishment, terrorism and constant crises had not made governing the country an almost impossible challenge, it would never have entered my head to take on the task."[16]

The Quixote quest has its proper animus and limitations. The quixotic hero never understands failure as the result of his own shortcomings. To him, failure always issues from the intractability of the world. Failure may even come from exhaustion; but never from the misplacement of emotions or the erroneous understanding of things. In his messianic moments, the quixotic hero may even understand failure as a fateful event. In that case, his self-proclaimed tragic effort confers on him nobility. In Peru, Vargas Llosa anticipated, all heroes so far have been defeated.[17]

THE STORYTELLER

From the troubadours of the *sertón* in Brazil to the Seanchaí of Ireland, Vargas Llosa has noted, the Storyteller is someone who rekindles the fire of collective memory. Like Walter Benjamin, he envisions the Storyteller as a transmitter of collective wisdom, hopes, and desires.[18]

Benjamin believed the Storyteller was a character of the past, a character whose voice was finally drowned by the metallic, impersonal noises of modernity. A man born in Peru, at the fringes of the modern world, in a land where *habladores* still make a living performing on the streets, cutting through the veil of ideology and custom, exposing collective wounds, raising a mirror to collective feelings and failings, Vargas Llosa believes the Storyteller has metamorphosed but endures.[19] Unlike Lukacs and Benjamin, who conceived of the novel as a bourgeois form par excellence and hence utterly allied with the powers of modernity against the dream-bird that hatched the egg of desire in more placid times, Vargas Llosa not only makes room for the Storyteller as a character in his literary creations, he aspires to be one himself.

COMMUNION

The strength of the vision of the Storyteller is grounded in the strength of his culture. The world beyond, threatening or becoming, must be appropriated through the webs of meaning particular to that culture. To be equal to his task, therefore, the Storyteller must find a home within his culture. His place need not be a coveted nor even a respected one; but it is indispensable that the Storyteller's audience stir under the impact of his words ricocheting in the deep recesses of a psychological communion. In this sense, the image of the Storyteller and that of the prophets of old—foretellers of disasters and admonishers of those unable or unwilling to follow the path of covenant and salvation—fuse into one.

A PERUVIAN STORYTELLER

Despite his repeated renunciations, Vargas Llosa is a Peruvian—not European—Storyteller. He draws strength from his own complex, if not damned, culture. Like prophets of old, he feels shame, anger, and pity for the barbarous land. But, by his own admission, he cannot remove the call of the land and its people from under his skin. He knows he must see the world through the prism of the culture that nurtured him to adulthood and bestowed upon him heaps of pain and shame. This is why, in one way or another, most of his major literary efforts are about Peru.[20] He feels that cursed land in his bones, and the more he looks to distance himself, the closer he draws to it emotionally, metaphysically. The telluric—a *huachafo* term—envelops him.

IDEALIZATIONS

Vargas Llosa has never offered a Good Lie about Europe or America. This is not because he really does not know Europe or America the way he knows his own land. Not only does he appear to have spent more time in Madrid, London, or Paris than in Loreto or Cusco, but inadequate knowledge has never been a serious deterrent to writing fiction. It is certainly not a deterrent to a quixotic hero. What to make, then, of the fact that Vargas Llosa feels free to write about Iquitos and the Andes critically without much apprehension of misrepresenting things, whereas his remarks on the shortcomings of Western culture, on the other hand, are proffered, here and there, muffled by care and deference? Why has he not—so far, at least— engaged, critically, the culture he so admires and to which he wishes to belong? Because like other Peruvians of his class, he idealizes those lands. Furthermore, as ideal-typical and utopic, they play a pivotal role in his posture as writer/Storyteller: the idealized West becomes his measuring rod for all that is human. An inability to imitate those Others is punishable by economic backwardness and political barbarism. Europe and America, it seems, play a role similar, though in reverse, to that of the Philistines in the ancient drama of the Jewish people.

REINVENTIONS

The role of the Storyteller/prophet could not be more difficult than in Peru—a cursed and chaotic land, inhabited by individuals embodying antagonistic cultures, languages, and values, and hence necessitating either the rule of a ruthless strongman or, perhaps, the gifts of a Storyteller, to bring order into chaos and unite individuals into a people, according to Vargas Llosa. In other words, as for some prophets of old, the task of the Storyteller in Peru is to invent a new identity, a new Truth, a new Nation. This means the Storyteller must reinterpret the past, understand the present ruthlessly, and, grounded on such insights, carry the project of reinvention forward into the future. Perhaps that was why Vargas Llosa entered politics, against his better judgment and seemingly against his own interests: in Peru, the Storyteller had to become a politico.

CHARISMA

In his discussions on charisma, Max Weber noted that the role of prophet cannot be enacted without the willingness to assent on the part of those for and to whom the charismatic leader speaks. When it comes to changing the world, prophets can only do so much. Similarly, the task of the writer/Storyteller is nearly impossible unless his culture has already woven into existence the expectation that culture bearers have not only the right but the duty to demand sacrifices and constancy in action even against overwhelming odds. Vargas Llosa believes such is the case in Latin America in general and Peru in particular. As a culture bearer, he has always felt he was being asked to be oracle, wisdom personified, priest, mentor, teacher, father, and caudillo. Reluctantly, he prepared himself to obey the demand.

Charisma, particularly in modern times, is very seldom transferable. Few great military leaders, for example, become elder statesmen or high priests. Few great writer/critics become presidents of their countries. This makes it remarkable that, on hearing the demands of his people, Vargas Llosa took a chance and advanced the claim. He did his best not to falter. He began by accepting that he was different from the Many. He accepted his condition as marginal man; perhaps an extraordinary man for extraordinary times. He declared himself prepared to show his mettle and, by his own account, endangered his life for the sake of the cause.[21] At the same time, he declared himself utterly attached to principles, a rebel against the up-to-then immoral ways of conducting public affairs. And, for a while, he had the ears and hearts of the Many, who seemed to appreciate his courage and sacrifices.

Then, perhaps because the Many saw the price of reinventing themselves as too high, or perhaps because it eventually became clear that the voice of the fabulist mingled freely with that of the statesman, that the evils he denounced were not as altogether intractable as he believed, that the hopes he offered were squalid in comparison to other long-standing hopes, that his dream of a prosperous land was based on a neoliberal ideology with all the limitations that reality visits upon all such constructions, the people walked away. In the end, his proclaimed self-immolation—neglect of his creative powers, distaste for pressing the flesh of the Many—was not sufficient to retain them.

THE INTRACTABLE WORLD

After the defeat, Vargas Llosa and his closest allies looked around for reasons. They were led to the recapitulation of old truths: the people are still like children.[22] They are credulous, steeped in myth and magic, hoping for a false messiah to save them, and easily led astray by would-be Storytellers who sacrifice the sacrosanct role for the sake of material rewards.[23] The writer/Storyteller had offered a truer language and self-immolation as an antidote to the weight of a twisted tradition. It was not enough. And so, his quixotic will spent, he claimed a role as eternal outsider. He would dispense counsel through his art; he might approximate the exemplary prophets of old. His defeat by the world had not produced a retreat but a return.

11

Two Foxes of Peru

Something identifies you with the one who pulls away from you, and it's the common faculty of returning: Thus your overwhelming grief.

Something separates you from the one who stays with you, and it's the common slavery of parting: thus your puny rejoicing.

—C. Vallejo[1]

TWO STORYTELLERS

In the context of postmodernity, it is difficult to hold fast to aesthetic comparisons. Beauty, like Truth, is relative; it resides in the murky eyes of an ever-changing and hence insubstantial ego. In this important sense, Vargas Llosa is not a postmodernist writer/critic. Rather, like modernists of old, he holds that there is indeed a distinction between greater and lesser works of art. The difference has largely to do, he notes, with the presence or absence of *elementos añadidos*: the contributions made by an author's imagination to the world at large.

On these grounds, Vargas Llosa considers José María Arguedas to be among the best of Peruvian writers. The *elemento añadido* that such a tragic writer contributed to the world is major: a utopic image of the archaic Andean world. The utopic vision translated a protest against the real world of the Andes, which Arguedas knew well and did not like. In this sense, argues Vargas Llosa, Arguedas stood on the shoulders of other great utopic writers such as Inca Garcilaso de la Vega and Antonio León Pinelo.[2] Arguedas's archaic utopia is an updated version of an old device of protest against an accommodation with an evil world; in this case, in the context of Peru's approximation to modernity.

INDIO SONQO AND WOULD-BE EUROPEAN

The valuation of the aesthetic production of both these writers is destined to change with time. Those who have witnessed their efforts are much too close to know now which author, or aesthetic product, will endure in the collective memory of the Peruvian people and for how long. Perhaps José María Arguedas's best novels will endure, despite what Vargas Llosa in his sympathetic and honest appraisal identifies as their formal failings, because in them the *indio sonqo* managed to capture, in an aesthetic vision, the fading world of a people. Perhaps in the best mytho-poetic pages of his novels future Peruvians will recognize the trapped echoes of what they once were, or might have been. If this is so, art would seem to endure not only because of its aesthetic value, its formal virtuosity, but also because, through it, the collective memories and desires of a people find enduring resonances.

As for Mario Vargas Llosa's art, there is no doubt it must be grouped with the very best that Latin America has produced in this century. His fictions are destined to endure as the high mark in aesthetic production during the turbulent days since the midcentury. Will future Peruvians care about the insights and visions of a mestizo man writing in the dismal days before the New World prefigured in his fiction? Does the staying power of his works depend, more than those of Arguedas, on what Borges considered the tradition, the language?[3] If so, does this mean they will survive as "good reads"? More likely: Arguedas's and Vargas Llosa's work will endure as the two inextricably connected faces of a Peru that changed forever during this century. These Storytellers, one from the highlands and the other from the coast, will survive or vanish together.

This is why, even now, it is possible to make some noninvidious comparisons. It is already useful to understand the lifework of both writers as indicators of a pulsating and ever-changing collective reality. Their work can be used as the occasion for reflecting on the trajectory of a people toward the possible futures prefigured in their aesthetic offerings. And, as we do this, we realize that no two other Peruvians have such opposite visions of what their cursed land has been, is, will be, or ought to be. Of course, whether they were in fact able to capture all possible futures with their imagination, only those yet to come can say.

BURNING BRIDGES

The parallels in the lives of these two great writers begin with the scars left on their souls by similar childhood experiences.

In his childhood and youth, Vargas Llosa demonstrates, Arguedas was marginal and marginalized.[4] He suffered under not only a cruel stepmother but also his much older stepbrother, who made him witness base sexual acts against defenseless women. That marginalization, which began as a cruel act by others, was eventually self-imposed. Arguedas retreated to the world of the Indians. His uncle's household servants first, and the members of a struggling but independent Indian community later, offered him solidarity and solace. But the scars were already too deep; they would influence his literature decisively.

As a writer and citizen, Vargas Llosa notes, Arguedas always felt close to, drawn by, those who suffer. As if driven by a compulsion to repeat, as if trying to work through earlier traumas by reliving them, Arguedas seems to have been captivated by the world of the unsightly.[5] But the efforts at exorcism were never successful. He never fully succeeded in seeing sexuality as something sublime, or a token of love, for example. It remained in his emotional lexicon as something violent, dirty; a polluting act.[6]

Eventually, Arguedas managed to escape this oppressive world. His internal exile took him to the Peruvian coast. He tried his best to fit in there, to gain the accoutrements of success. He accomplished that to a high degree. But he never really felt at home there. To the end of his life, Arguedas felt like an outsider in a mestizo world that had learned to adulate him. Perhaps because of these experiences, Arguedas's memory of having belonged in an Indian community in the highlands was not so much a recollection of fact as a necessary personal myth. Perhaps Vargas Llosa is right: the invention of an archaic world was for José María Arguedas at once protest and crutch.

TRAUMAS

Vargas Llosa also suffered scars during his childhood. From very early on, taught by experience, young Mario learned to see his father as an oppressor. And from his public confessions, it appears the relationship between his mother and father was, at times, violent. A sensitive child, he could not have been other than traumatized. More generally, in a thoroughly machista world, his sensitive soul was surely a source of constant pain. Being thought effeminate appears to have gained him the unwelcome sexual attention of a priest and an internship in a pre-military academy. Young Mario was bombarded with the unremitting demand that he deny himself.

To survive, like countless other sensitive souls, young Mario learned to simulate and dissimulate. The aesthetic daemon grew, at least in large part, as a ray of hope in a world of shadows. Much as Arguedas had done, Vargas Llosa turned for solace to personal mythology. He invented the world of Miraflores as the closest approximation to paradise. Eventually, he would turn his back on Peru in exchange for greater solace. But during those fateful days of childhood, his dismal experiences may have affected even his conception of love: it appears no accident that his enduring emotional relations have developed within the safe and warm circles of his extended tribe.

Like Arguedas, Vargas Llosa also went into exile. In his case, it meant leaving Peru altogether. And here, the parallels strain. For, unlike Arguedas, Vargas Llosa seems never to have felt he had left a paradise behind. Whatever paradise Vargas Llosa learned to cherish abroad, it was an invention nestled in the future and outside Peru. Even Miraflores could not but pale by comparison to such a utopia. In fact, once he had become successful on the other shore, his disdain for what he had left behind only grew. Peru could then only offer a field of action against which to measure an amending will. And yet, Vargas Llosa confesses that, after all these years, like Arguedas, he has not been able to exorcise the pull the cursed land has on him; his inspiration runs truly free only when he writes about Peru. This failed exorcism means that, like Arguedas, Vargas Llosa is attracted to misery and muck, to a land he has tried to forsake.

COMMITMENTS

Arguedas wished to be a committed Storyteller.[7] He followed in the tradition of the Latin American writer. But his commitment was very particular: he wished to speak for the Indian people. In this sense, he might be considered an Indigenista writer who embraced Justice as his master virtue. His membership in the Indigenista movement was nuanced, however. He was never comfortable with either of the two core solutions to the so-called Indian Problem offered by the movement: liberal or socialist. He knew that, ultimately, neither of the two competing ideologies could or would accommodate, or even tolerate, the Indian.[8] Lacking a viable alternative, he opted for socialism as the lesser of two evils. He thought it provided the best opportunity for Indians to retain their sense of self as they entered modernity. Vargas Llosa is right: Arguedas often wished the Indian could remain unchanged, even in the face of rapidly changing circumstances.

Arguedas wished to tell a good story. In this sense, too, he was different from most Indigenista writers. The aesthetic daemon, to use Vargas Llosa's terms, had settled deep within his soul. Still, what truly animated Arguedas was not to write the best novel. He aimed to offer an insight into a complex and valuable culture he saw fading from memory. Arguedas conceived of art as a way of knowing. His fictions were meant as contributions to reflecting on a part of Peru systematically denied by whites and mestizos. His best work, like all great art, was didactic. The weaving of a good story did not exhaust the aesthetic effort. In Arguedas, the Indigenista and the aesthetic animus coincide. He saw accomplished art as a means to something else.

TENDENTIOUSNESS

Vargas Llosa insists that he conceives of his literary works first and foremost as aesthetic products. Art is an end-in-itself. As we have seen, his attention to form and its aesthetic effects is such that he is willing to sacrifice just about anything and everything to that end. If it is true, as he claims, that he does not choose his daemons, that they overwhelm him, it is also true that he sees such daemons as ultimately grounded in the very personal and all-too-human. They are far from translating the silent, weighty demands of a fading people.

This understanding of art and of self is lived in the context of a complex world, of course. In that world, "nadie sabe para quien trabaja": no one knows the vicissitudes awaiting egos and their creations. On the one hand, honesty in self-understanding and artistic commitment does not dull the impact of that world upon the self and its products. On the other, self-proclaimed aloofness and the circumscription of art do not preclude their effects on the world. For many in Peru and around the world, Vargas Llosa's art has always been tendentious. When the tendency was clearly to the left, even the author acknowledged it as such. Literature was then equated with fire. When the tendency turned to the right, the author effected a cautious return to a conception of art as an independent sphere of action. Through it all, however, Vargas Llosa's literature has provided the occasion for reflecting on the past, the present, and the future of his native land. This is why Vargas Llosa and Arguedas stand together, perhaps despite themselves.

VISIONS OF MODERNITY

There are significant differences in these two writers' attitudes to the events of their times. Arguedas viewed the modern world with great suspicion. Much like Miguel Angel Asturias, that other rescuer of fading traditions, he believed that not only the Indian but the mestizo culture of Latin America as well was in danger of disappearing under the clutter of clocks, robots, computers, and money. The encounter between Spain and the so-called New World was terrible; but its effects were limited to the replacement of one cosmic vision for another. Defeated and badly injured, the Indian could retreat into adopted and reworked spiritual temples. The effects of the encounter with the onslaught of clocks and robots made possible by the Cultural Industry, however, might be the undermining, the erasing, of the soul itself.[9] This is why it is important, Arguedas offered with his life, that Indian traditions be nurtured into the future; they might be our only adequate antidote to the disenchantment of the world. And for Vargas Llosa, this was one of Arguedas's main weaknesses, both as a writer and as a citizen. He let despair rule his vision; he let his fictive universe enter his quotidian life. And vice versa. The hoped-for antidote is pure fiction. Being a realist himself, Vargas

Llosa refuses to place his hopes on Indian shoulders. Instead, he aims to look at his world devoid of illusions. And so he presents us with a world without asymptotes for living, without possible respite from lies and deception; a world inhabited by amoral and shifty *vivos* who, as a byproduct of their ignorance, end up inviting totalitarian rulers such as Alberto Fujimori.[10] If Arguedas told the story of the unsightly to show us their humanity, Vargas Llosa tells the same story to show us our inhumanity.[11]

COMMUNITY AND SOCIETY

The German historian and sociologist Ferdinand Tönnies wrote down the fundamental distinction Europeans sensed existed between life lived within a *Gemeinschaft* (community) and within a *Gesellschaft* (society).[12] The polar concepts were meant to underscore the trajectory of European societies from simple to complex. *Gemeinschaft* was a thing of the past; *Gesellschaft* was the way of the future. For the Western sociotheoretical tradition, the distinction was as fundamental as was Sarmiento's fateful distinction between Civilization and Barbarism for Latin Americans. But the valuations associated with the concepts were quite different. Ferdinand Toennies, like Max Weber, glanced back to the past with a tinge of nostalgia: life in a *Gemeinschaft* meant a warmer, more humane existence.

Émile Durkheim developed the extreme ideal types devoid of such nostalgia. For him, mechanical-solidarity-based societies were simple, oppressive to developing individuals, quite brittle and hence unable to adapt to changing circumstances, dependent on magic and myth, averse to Science as the fullest exemplification of Reason, close to the earth and hence to herd life, and having penal laws based on sentiment as the main cohesive glue. By contrast, organic-solidarity-based societies are complex, nurture the full development of the individual, have gained independence from nature through Science, and rely for their cohesion on rationally constituted laws. Only humans who live in such societies are ready to take on Science as their god-term and dare to replace God.[13]

TRADITION AND MODERNITY

In the creation of his utopic Ideal Type, José María Arguedas went beyond Toennies: within their fading communities, Indians found identity and communion and hence were never lost to themselves; ritual humanized nature, and nature welcomed humans into her bosom; deep feelings were sure guides for leading a good life. The Ideal Type of the antipode was also starkly drawn: modern society is a whirlpool where humans lose their souls, Science passes for Reason, money—as Marx had noted in his youth—is the universal whore, and evil parades in civilized garb.

In the creation of his distopic Ideal Type of community, Vargas Llosa goes beyond Durkheim: the archaic world was hierarchical, brittle, brutal, oppressive, unpredictable, and evil. In his Ideal Type of the antipode he draws closer to Durkheim: the capitalist world enhances our independence from nature; it nurtures the Individual as a good over against Community; it establishes the supremacy of Reason; it develops the Market and creates wealth; in using money as the universal medium of exchange it fosters Freedom. It is good to be a capitalist.[14]

CONTRADICTIONS

Despite the distopic Ideal Type, Arguedas believed that a New Peru was being forged in the middle of this century. This was a mestizo Peru; in tune with progressive developments around the world; where humans could live all *patrias*; that is, enjoy all life-affirming cultural traditions. Arguedas committed suicide in 1969, not because he saw the future of Peru as dismal, but because he believed he could not participate effectively in its construction. He did not manage to transform his social optimism into a private reason for carrying on.

Vargas Llosa insists: "lo peruano no existe": there is nothing that can be said to be proper to Peruvians.[15] Much of his fiction and critical work is dedicated to demonstrating that fact. In his vision, Peru is an *entrevero*, a variegation of disparate and distrusting races and ethnicities inhabiting disconnected regions and possessing dissimilar languages and histories. But he also insists, vehemently: Peruvians have a tendency to self-pity, they exhibit a victim's mentality fraught with a latent masochism and a deep sense of resentment.[16] All of this has produced a society of liars, cheaters, *vivos*, and *pendejos*.[17]

THE RECEDING APOCALYPSE

Arguedas and Vargas Llosa share in an apocalyptic vision of the future of Peru.[18] For Arguedas, the apocalypse was drawing nearer as a revolutionary movement, prefiguring the birth of a new society where the Indian might find his own place in the sun. As in nature, destruction renews life. For Vargas Llosa, the coming apocalypse brings only destruction. Faced with that, the only hope for Peruvians is to become Other; to follow the path of the *informales*; to embrace the Market; to forge a new society free from archaic utopias; to exhibit virile maturity.

The apocalyptic fears have subsided over the last few years in Peru. Peruvians seem determined to learn to live with chaos—that of the market included. If Vargas Llosa is right and literature flourishes when the social conditions are dismal, let us hope that he and those Storytellers to come find inspiration in less dramatic possibilities. But let us also hope that the promise hosted in Arguedas's apocalyptic vision does not fade away unfulfilled and, worse yet, unnoticed.

Epilogue

Mario Vargas Llosa's extant canon evidences oscillations and contradictions regarding fundamental moral and conceptual problems engaged by the Western sociotheoretical tradition. He sees Individual Freedom as a value-in-itself, for example, while upholding the right of Society to curb its members' proclivities; he advocates respect for rules, while celebrating their stubborn transgression.

The oscillations and contradictions in his sociotheoretical thinking have so far made it impossible for Vargas Llosa to offer his readers a unified moral or conceptual system. In this he stands a fair distance from many of the leading intellectuals of the nineteenth century in Europe, who strove to grasp the manifold of experience in one overarching conceptual schema. His steadfast celebration of radical artistic freedom seems to have inoculated him against the hubris of trying to provide a total system. In truth, even the Total Novel was only a substitution; it was a sublimation of the urge to replace God. Indeed, when it comes to moral and social concerns, Mario Vargas Llosa's offering is best appreciated as the efforts of a bricoleur.

The eclectic approach of a bricoleur makes possible the seemingly easy coexistence of quite different conceptual and value positions. For if Vargas Llosa's replacement of Sartre for Camus and Marx for Popper could be understood as the result of wisdom born of historical experiences, his current embrace of ideas from such disparate thinkers as Karl Popper, Albert Camus, Isaiah Berlin, and Milton Friedman seems quite superficial. This impression has little to do with Vargas Llosa's desire or ability to distill the best of each of his authors' offerings and make them his own. Rather, it is because the bricoleur cannot but do violence to the material with which he attempts to fashion his precarious world.

The eclectic approach has strengths. Minimally, it is not dogmatic in its inclusionary dimensions and hence makes possible profiting from the wealth of human experiences. In this sense, the bricoleur and the writer of fictions are soul mates. When it comes to pursuing the world-historical tasks of the Latin American writer, however, the eclectic posture shows marked shortcomings. The task of the Storyteller there, for example, is to provide his audience glimpses of an integrated, meaningful universe—even if it is only an invention based on dimly understood desires. Such is the necessary backdrop for his counsel. By contrast and by experience, the bricoleur can only offer the insight that nothing is secure in the world; that the limits of our imagination are the limits of our possibilities; that the whirlwind of change ushers in Chaos as king. Such a Storyteller cannot hold the attention of his audiences for long.

The conception of the Market is meant to take care of these and related problems for Vargas Llosa, the would-be world-historical leader. In the unified field of Market forces, Chaos is to produce goodness and competition, peace. But, it turns out, the Market has always been, and continues to be, parasitic. It keeps on going by borrowing strength from such virtues as Freedom, Truthfulness, Justice, and Tolerance. And, at least thus far, such virtues have always been grounded in the trust and fear of God's will.

Will Mario Vargas Llosa, as would-be world-historical leader, remain a bricoleur and hold fast to radical freedom? Will he end up embracing a will-bending ideology, such as religion? Or will he continue, honestly and hence precariously, straddling the realm of Freedom and the realm of Necessity? Only time will tell.

Notes

CHAPTER 1

1. See Berel Lang, ed., *The Death of Art* (New York: Haven Publications, 1984); Arthur Coleman Danto, *After the End of Art: Contemporary Art and the Pale of History* (Princeton: Princeton University Press, 1997).

2. See Georg Lukacs, *The Theory of the Novel: A Historico-Philosophical Essay on the Forms of Great Epic Literature* (Cambridge: MIT Press, 1968); Hans-Georg Gadamer, *Truth and Method* (New York: Seabury Press, 1975).

3. Mario Vargas Llosa, *Contra viento y marea II (1972–1983)* (Barcelona: Seix Barral, 1986), 423; *Espejo de escritores*, notas y prólogo de Reina Roff (Hanover: Ediciones del Norte, 1985), 158–59.

4. See Vargas Llosa, *Contra viento y marea II*, 21, 24, 134; "The Boom Twenty Years Later: An Interview with Mario Vargas Llosa," *Latin American Literary Review* 5, no. 29 (1987): 204.

5. All other daemons—politics, economics, religion, science, sexuality—are competitor daemons who cannot be catered to without betraying literature. Like Weber, too, Vargas Llosa finds two daemons particularly detrimental to his own: politics and religion. See Mario Vargas Llosa, *El buitre y el ave fenix: conversaciones con Mario Vargas Llosa* (Barcelona: Editorial Anagrana, 1972), 25; *Semana de autor: Mario Vargas Llosa* (Madrid: Ediciones Cultura Hispánica, Instituto de Cooperación Iberoamericana, 1985), 40; *Contra viento y marea I (1962–1972)* (Barcelona: Seix Barral, 1983), 117, 133, 258; "Una insurrección permanente," *Marcha*, no. 1294 (1966): 108. For Max Weber's classic statement, see "Science as a Vocation," in *From Max Weber: Essays in Sociology* (New York: Oxford University Press, 1946).

6. See Mario Vargas Llosa, preface to *Kathie y el hipopótamo* (Barcelona: Seix Barral, 1983),11; *Contra viento y marea II*, 424; *La Verdad de las mentiras* (Barcelona: Seix Barral, 1990), 192.

7. See Lukacs, *The Theory of the Novel*; Ian Watts, *The Rise of the Novel: Studies in DeFoe, Richardson, and Fielding* (Berkeley: University of California Press, 1957); Braulio Muñoz, *Sons of the Wind: The Search for Identity in Spanish American Indian Literature* (New Brunswick: Rutgers University Press, 1983), translated into the Spanish by Nancy K. Muñoz, as *Huairapamushcas: la búsqueda de la identidad en la novela indigenista hispanoamericana*, with a new introduction (Temuco: Ediciones de la Universidad de la Frontera, 1996); Octavio Paz, *El arco y la lira.* (México, D.F.: Fondo de Cultura Económica, 1956); Vargas Llosa, *Contra viento y marea I*, 274.

8. See Vargas Llosa, *El buitre y el ave fenix*, 51; Mario Vargas Llosa, *García Márquez: historia de un deicidio* (Barcelona: Barral Editores, 1971), 86; Mario Vargas Llosa, *Historia de Mayta* (Barcelona: Seix Barral, 1984), 91.

9. It is in this sense, for example, that Vargas Llosa considers José María Arguedas among the best of Peruvian writers, despite what he sees as the technical flaws in his work. See Mario Vargas Llosa, *La utopía arcaica: José María Arguedas y las ficciones del indigenismo* (México, D.F.: Fondo de Cultura Económica, 1996); Mario Vargas Llosa, *Contra viento y marea I*, 47; Mario Vargas Llosa, *La orgía perpetua: Flaubert y "Madame Bovary"* (Madrid: Taurus, 1975), 147, 259.

10. Vargas Llosa, *La orgía perpetua*, 276; *Contra viento y marea II*, 424.

11. See Vargas Llosa, *La orgía perpetua*, 163, 267, 268. Vargas Llosa claims to take sides with Flaubert against Brecht on this point. Brecht writes in such a way, Vargas Llosa says, that "in practice, he appears to presuppose an infantilism or ineptitude on the part of his readers: everything must be explained and underlined for them so as not to give them the least opportunity to make a mistake, to misinterpret." *La orgía perpetua*, 267. (All translations from the Spanish are mine, unless otherwise indicated.) This understanding of Brecht's work is debatable. It could be argued, as did Theodor Adorno, for example, that it is precisely in the practice of his art that Brecht frees himself from the self-imposed straight-jacket of ideology. See "Commitment," *New Left Review*, no. 87/88 (1974): 75–89. Additionally, it must be noted that to steer clear of overt didacticism is easier said than done. Even in the case of Vargas Llosa himself, who must be counted among the most self-reflective about his craft, it is difficult not to see his apocalyptic novels, such as *Historia de Mayta* and *Lituma en los Andes* (Barcelona: Planeta, 1993), as didactic and ideological. For an interesting treatment of the subject, see Lucién Goldmann, *Le dieu cache: étude sur la vision tragique dans les Pensées de Pascal et dans le théâtre de Racine* (Paris, Gallimard, 1955).

CHAPTER 2

1. Quoted by Georg Lukacs, *The Theory of the Novel: A Historico-Philosophical Essay on the Forms of Great Epic Literature* (Cambridge: MIT Press, 1968), 87.

2. Michel Foucault attributes Nietzsche's insight to his philologist's knack. It was Nietzsche, he argued, who made a clearing for the rebirth of daemons. See Michel Foucault, *The Order of Things: An Archaeology of the Human Sciences* (New York: Vintage Books, 1970), 306. Nietzsche's daring effort had a high price. He celebrated the rebirth of the gods at the same time he celebrated biology as a Thing-In-Itself. The adjudicatory element in his hoped-for world was power: the power of the strong over the weak. The history of Europe before and during World War II was the dismal coda to a philosophy of life shared by many, and Nietzsche had the honesty to articulate this.

3. The clearest explanation of this idea is to be found in *García Márquez: historia de un deicidio*, but it is also discussed throughout his earlier writings. See Mario Vargas Llosa, *Contra viento y marea I (1962–1972)* (Barcelona: Seix Barral, 1983), 233–34; *García Márquez: historia de un deicidio* (Barcelona: Barral Editores, 1971), 101; *La orgía perpetua: Flaubert y "Madame Bovary"* (Madrid: Taurus, 1975),148.

4. See, for example, M. Keith Booker, *Vargas Llosa among the Postmodernists* (Gainsville: University of Florida Press, 1994).

5. Answering Angel Rama's characterization of his theories as "nineteenth-century," Vargas Llosa notes that he used the term daemon instead of obsession because he did not wish to convey an overly psychological understanding of the matter. The clarification does not go far enough. Since its inception, psychology has oscillated between a spiritualist and a materialist tendency. See *Contra viento y marea I*, 263.

6. The connection between creativity and sexuality is quite clear in Vargas Llosa's theories. In *La tía Julia y el escribidor*, Camacho, a partial alter ego for the author, puts it bluntly: "Women and art exclude one another, my friend. In every vagina an artist is buried." Mario Vargas Llosa, *La tía Julia y el escribidor* (Barcelona: Seix Barral, 1977), 193. He quotes with admiration Flaubert's conception of the literary act: "the only way to stand our existence is to immerse ourselves in literature as in a perpetual orgy." *La orgía perpetua*, 91. And he confesses that the erotic literature he read as a youth was influential in his later creative process. See Mario Vargas Llosa, *El pez en el agua: memorias* (Barcelona: Seix Barral, 1993), 336. This conception of the erotic and art is clearly associated with the notion that the artistic creation is guided, pushed along by unconscious motivations. See Vargas Llosa, *Contra viento y marea I*, 233.

7. Thus, he argues that García Márquez "invented his cultural tradition, according to his own personal and historical daemons. Hence the chaos of sources, the inconceivable mixtures, the fusion of such disparate elements." Vargas Llosa, *García Márquez: historia*, 206. He writes of *El coronel no tiene quien le escriba*, "The daemons that now urged him to write, those experiences that he wished to rescue and exorcise, had an objective, external and historical nature: social injustice, political repression and corruption, misery, hunger, the effects that in a collectivity have such events as revolution and war." Vargas Llosa, *García Márquez: historia*, 152. He makes similar points regarding the works of José María Arguedas. See Mario Vargas Llosa, *La utopía arcaica: José María Arguedas y las ficciones del indigenismo* (México, D.F.: Fondo de Cultura Económica, 1996). It is not only Latin American authors, heirs to such accidented history, who are thus influenced by cultural daemons. European authors such as Coleridge, argues Vargas Llosa, feel the same forces. Vargas Llosa, *García Márquez: historia*, 205.

8. See Lukacs, *The Theory of the Novel*; Hans-Georg Gadamer, *Truth and Method* (New York: Seabury Press, 1975)

9. Indigenismo was a social, political, and literary movement (~1919–64) that swept Latin America, calling for the liberation of the Indian and his culture. Members of the movement used literature as a critical/political tool and considered its aesthetic aspects of secondary importance. The best novel written in the Indigenista tradition is *Los rios profundos* by José María Arguedas (Buenos Aires: Editorial Losada, 1958). An analysis of the Indigenista literature as a whole shows that, even though the manifest aim of the movement was to redeem the Indian, the hidden desire of most authors was the destruction of the Indian culture. See Braulio Muñoz, *Sons of the Wind: The Search for Identity in Spanish American Indian Literature* (New Brunswick: Rutgers University Press, 1983).

10. See, in this connection, Julio Ortega, *Crítica de la identidad: la pregunta por el Perú en su literatura* (México, D.F.: Fondo de Cultura Económica, 1988).

11. This notion of the demands of art has a long history. Even Karl Marx, for example, embraced it. He envisioned the move from the realm of Necessity to the realm of Freedom as a move from forced to free labor. But contrary to an anarchist interpretation of the move, Marx conceived of the creative act as a most serious and difficult task. "Really free working, e.g., composing, is at the same time precisely the most damned seriousness, the

most intense exertion." Karl Marx, *Gründrisse: Foundations of the Critique of Political Economy* (New York: Vintage Books, 1973), 611.

12. Vargas Llosa's conception of the novel as a critique of reality could be misunderstood if we take "critique" to mean a leftist critique. His notion of critique is not exhausted by the moral-political valuations attributed to the term during the sixties, which made it seem as though all critique has to be paired with a positive appraisal of the socialism-democracy-freedom complex. In Latin America, the critique of the subjective and social worlds has been developed by the right and the left. In his current phase, Vargas Llosa is following in the footsteps of such conservative writer/critics as Sarmiento and Borges.

13. At least up to 1981, when he published *La guerra del fin del mundo*, Vargas Llosa believed that for the author to achieve invisibility, it is necessary that he be impartial with regard to the happenings in the fictive world. See, for example, Martin de Riquer and Mario Vargas Llosa, *El combate imaginario: las cartas de batalla de Joanot Martorell* (Barcelona: Seix Barral, 1972), 23; and Vargas Llosa, *La orgía perpetua*, 103. More recently, the distinction between author and narrator has become blurred as biography and politics mingle freely in the aesthetic vision.

14. The way magico-realism, both as a technique and as a philosophy of life in Latin America, is dealt with by Vargas Llosa can help illustrate the way the Total Novel is supposed to approach the past: like most Latin Americans, Vargas Llosa believes that the fantastic has formed an important aspect of the subjective and objective reality among Latin Americans from the very beginning. (Perhaps such an attitude toward life was born of the fateful confluence of Spanish and Native American magico-mystical approaches to life and the cosmos.) In the Latin American literary tradition, the fantastic-magical-mythical complex has been displayed in a variety of ways, from the early chroniclers' feverish confessions to the poetry of the fantastic. More recently, this aspect of Latin American reality has been most fully displayed in the works of García Márquez. The upshot of García Márquez's success is that his version of magico-realism has become an essential part of the indispensable magma for the Latin American literary tradition. See Vargas Llosa, *García Márquez: historia de un deicidio*. In his own fiction, Vargas Llosa has shown this magico-realist tradition admirably, though his treatment of it is not as sympathetic as that of García Márquez. See, for example, Mario Vargas Llosa, *La casa verde* (Barcelona: Seix Barral,1966), 137; Mario Vargas Llosa, *Lituma en los Andes* (Barcelona: Planeta, 1993).

CHAPTER 3

1. Nietzsche used the term to designate a new breed of philosophers: free-spirited men whom he saw rising to question everything. See Friedrich Nietzsche, *Beyond Good and Evil: Prelude to a Philosophy of the Future* (New York: Vintage Books, 1966).

2. This dismissal is imperative for a postmodernist stance since there are cultures around the world that contradict its main position concerning such foundational notions as Truth or Beauty. To truly acknowledge such claims, a postmodernist intellectual would have to pare down his or her own perspective and relativize it. Postmodernism cannot survive the acknowledgment.

3. For an interesting treatment of the subject see Albert Memmi, *The Colonizer and the Colonized* (Boston: Beacon Press, 1965).

4. For an extensive treatment of the desire to belong to the universal culture, see Braulio Muñoz, *Sons of the Wind: The Search for Identity in Spanish American Indian Literature* (New Brunswick: Rutgers University Press, 1983), chapter 1.

5. See Braulio Muñoz, "On Relativity, Relativism, and Social Theory," in *Rationality, Relativism and the Human Sciences*, ed. Joseph Margolis, Michael Krausz, and R. M. Burian (Dordrecht, Netherlands: Martinus Nijhoff Publishers, 1986).

6. See Augusto Salazar Bondy, *Lima la horrible* (México, D.F.: Biblioteca ERA, 1964), 96.

7. See Memmi, *The Colonizer*; Octavio Paz, *El laberinto de la soledad* (México, D.F.: Fondo de Cultura Económica, 1963).

8. Salazar Bondy writes: "In praise of their knavery, the *vivos* deserve indulgence. The others, those who behave according to their conscience or the law, are *tontos*. Within the manicheistic psychology of the creoles, humanity is divided into *vivos* and *tontos*." *Lima la horrible*, 28–29.

9. See Mario Vargas Llosa, *La verdad de las mentiras* (Barcelona: Seix Barral, 1990), 19.

10. It is not only for their own benefit that the Good Europeans must polish their Lies—they must be careful not to become one of Salazar Bondy's *vivos*—but also for the sake of Society. Vargas Llosa writes: "The feigning attitude is indispensable to secure social coexistence, a social formation that, even though it appears hollow and forced from the perspective of the individual, takes on weight and substance from the point of view of the community. . . . If human beings were, like Meursault, pure instinct, not only would the family disappear but also society in general, and men would end up killing each other in the same banal and absurd way that Meursault kills the Arab on the beach." "El extranjero debe morir," in *La verdad de las mentiras*, 129.

11. See, in this connection, Mario Vargas Llosa, preface to *Kathie y el hipopótamo* (Barcelona: Seix Barral, 1983), 11; *Contra viento y marea II (1972–1983)* (Barcelona: Seix Barral, 1986), 418, 422; *La orgía perpetua: Flaubert y "Madame Bovary"* (Madrid: Taurus, 1975), 175; *La verdad de las mentiras*, 6.

12. There is a kind of tacit agreement between author and reader: the writer lets the Truth out tangentially, while the reader acknowledges it but feels free to dismiss it as mere fiction. Vargas Llosa notes this tacit knowledge in *La utopía arcáica: José María Arguedas y las ficciones del Indigenismo* (México D.F.: Fondo de Cultura Económica, 1996). See also *Kathie y el hipopótamo*, 9; *La verdad de las mentiras*, 126.

13. Vargas Llosa, *La verdad de las mentiras*, 19–20.

14. Vargas Llosa treats this subject in *El hablador*. Among the Machiguengas, lies are communal constructions. The fictive history offered by Mascarita partially quenches the Machiguengas' appetite for necessary Lies and thus enters the collective dream-work: "The man who harangues, before his enraptured audience, who would he be but that character who, from time immemorial, has been in charge of stoking the curiosity, fantasy, memory, desire for dreaming and lying of the machiguenga people?" *El hablador* (Barcelona: Seix Barral, 1987), 228.

15. A family scene in *Conversación en La Catedral:* "Delicious Mamá, of course he wanted more, was she stripping you like the prawns? Yes Mamá. An actor, Zavalita, a machiavellian, a cynic? Yes he would bring his laundry to be washed by the girls, Mamá. One who unfolded himself so many times it was impossible to know who he really was? Yes he would come to dinner every Sunday, Mamá. A victim or one more victimizer fighting tooth and nail to devour and not be devoured, one more Peruvian bourgeois? Yes he

would call by phone if he needed something, Mamá. Good in his house with his children, immoral in business, a political opportunist, no less nor more than others? Impotent with his wife, insatiable with his mistresses, lowering his pants in front of his driver?" Mario Vargas Llosa, *Conversación en La Catedral* (Barcelona: Seix Barral, 1971), 412.

16. From *La tía Julia*: "'What,' aunt Julia said, 'Not my sister, not my brother-in-law, not one of your kin made me suspect they knew and that they detested me. Always so affectionate with me, those hypocrites.'" Mario Vargas Llosa, *La tía Julia y el escribidor* (Barcelona: Seix Barral, 1977), 179.

17. "No te fíes ni de tu madre." Vargas Llosa, *Conversación en La Catedral*, 513.

18. From *Historia de Mayta*: "When I go to sleep I hear, at last, a rhythmic sound. No, it is not the night birds; it is the wind, that splashes against the terrace of the inn the water of Poca lagoon. That soft music and the beautiful starry sky of the nights in Jauja suggest a peaceful country, of reconciled and happy people. They lie, same as fiction." Mario Vargas Llosa, *Historia de Mayta* (Barcelona: Seix Barral, 1984), 307.

19. Vargas Llosa celebrates the noble and perilous task of literature in its battle against the morass of the mundane. His position is most clearly articulated in his critical essays, but it is also an important part of his fiction. Often, as in *Historia de Mayta* (20, 77, 336), he offers his vision of the role of literature in a fiction within fiction, where the invented world provides soothing respite from the oppressive fictive "real" reality. The point is stated quite straighforwardly in *Kathie y el hipopótamo*. Santigo: "The truth is that for quite a while I've also liked the make-believe and that these two short hours, of lies that become truths, of truths that are lies, also help me to better tolerate the remaining hours of the day" (141). In some cases, Vargas Llosa develops the writer as a character who attempts to gain freedom from the constraint of a common Lie by speaking the Truth to fictive readers. In *Historia de Mayta*, for example, the noble task of the writer is presented as the visceral need of an author to make sense of a chaotic, apocalyptic world, devoid of asymptotes for moral action. Free from the mundane lies through his imagination, the fictive writer sees the world for what it really is — a mess of fictive realities, half-truths, and all-too-human constructions — and attempts to articulate such Truth in the only way available to him: the novel form. Fiction and the writer of fiction are thus presented as providing the only respite from the chaos of a world abandoned by God. In other cases, characters grasp the Truth behind the Lies of the Many and abandon that oppressive world for another they invent. This is the case of Mascarita in *El hablador*. In part, he says, he turned his back on urban civilization because "We learned quickly, of course, the tricks, the cunning, the knavish deceits or graciousness needed to obtain, not even a privilege, but, to barely do with a minimum of decency that for which they paid us." *El hablador*, 146.

20. See Mario Vargas Llosa, *Contra viento y marea I (1962–1972)* (Barcelona: Seix Barral, 1983), 327–28.

21. See Mario Vargas Llosa, *La historia secreta de una novela* (Barcelona: Tusquets, 1971), 70; *Contra viento y marea II*, 191; *El pez en el agua: memorias*, (Barcelona: Seix Barral, 1993), 251, 361.

22. See Mario Vargas Llosa, *El pez en el agua* 184–85.

23. In José Miguel Oviedo, *Mario Vargas Llosa: la invención de una realidad* (Barcelona: Seix Barral, 1982), 247.

24. Julia Urquidi, Vargas Llosa's aunt by marriage who became lover, wife, and finally accuser, writes that, as part of the Llosa clan, she had learned to lie and to dissimulate like

everyone else; because she had learned that in the Peru of Odría and later dictators, "with friends one can get anything." She expected no less from her nephew and gleefully joined him in spinning little and bigger lies. See Julia Urguidi, *My Life with Mario Vargas Llosa*, trans. C. R. Perricone and Peter Lang (New York: American Studies Press, 1988), 61, 228.

25. See Vargas Llosa, *Contra viento y marea II*, 101; *El pez en el agua*, 309.

26. See Vargas Llosa, *El pez en el agua*, 492.

27. See Vargas Llosa, *El pez en el agua*, 261.

28. See Vargas Llosa, *El pez en el agua*, 396.

29. As a journalist, adduces Vargas Llosa, Gabriel García Márquez goes after the news with passion. If he does not find what he is looking for, he invents it. Mario Vargas Llosa, *García Márquez: historia de un deicidio* (Barcelona: Seix Barral Editores, 1971), 41.

30. The "Informe sobre Uchuraccay" was presented to President Belaunde Terry in March 1983. See Mario Vargas Llosa, *Contra viento y marea III (1964–1988)* (Barcelona: Seix Barral, 1990), 101, 182. Outside Peru, the report was seen as an interesting installment of Vargas Llosa's phenomenal literary output. In America, it appeared in the Sunday magazine section of the *New York Times*. His presentation of the long-standing scission between Civilization and Barbarism played well among Western audiences as exotica. It is interesting to note that the voices of the *comuneros* of Uchuraccay are never heard in this report. Their positions are conveyed through the third person plural and in indirect speech. For a very interesting, thorough analysis of the report, see Enrique Meyer, "Peru in Deep Trouble: Mario Vargas Llosa's 'Inquest in the Andes' Reexamined," *Cultural Anthropology* 6, no. 4 (1991): 466–504.

31. See Braulio Muñoz, "Law-Givers: From Plato to Freud and Beyond," *Theory, Culture and Society* 6 (1989). See also Braulio Muñoz, *Tensions in Social Theory: Groundwork for a Future Moral Sociology* (Chicago: Loyola University Press, 1993).

CHAPTER 4

1. See Mario Vargas Llosa, *La verdad de las mentiras* (Barcelona: Seix Barral, 1990), 22; "Comedia de equivocaciones," in *América Latina: marca registrada* (Buenos Aires: Grupo Editorial Zeta, S.A., 1992), 110.

2. See Vargas Llosa, "Comedia de equivocaciones," 121–22.

3. See Max Weber, *The Protestant Ethic and the Spirit of Capitalism* (New York: Charles Scribner's Sons, 1958); Robert K. Merton, *The Sociology of Science: Theoretical and Empirical Investigations*, ed. and with an introduction by Norman W. Storer (Chicago: University of Chicago Press, 1973); Robert K. Merton, *Science, Technology and Society in Seventeenth-Century England* (New York: H. Fertig, 1970).

4. See, for example, Charles H. Lippy, *Modern American Popular Religion: A Critical Assessment and Annotated Bibliography* (Westport, Conn.: Greenwood Press, 1996); Martin E. Marty, ed., *New and Intense Movements*, with an introduction by Martin E. Marty (Munich, New York: K. G. Saur, 1992); Martin E. Marty and R. Scott Appleby, eds., *Fundamentalisms and Society: Reclaiming the Sciences, the Family, and Education* (Chicago: University of Chicago Press, 1993).

5. See Vargas Llosa, *La verdad de las mentiras*, 49, 123. As has been intimated before, Vargas Llosa's love for his country is quite complex. He has written, for example: "It is

important that everyone understands once and for all: the more severe the writings of an author against his country are the more intense is the passion that unites him to it. Because in the domain of literature violence is a proof of love." Mario Vargas Llosa, *Contra viento y marea I (1962–1972)* (Barcelona: Seix Barral, 1983), 179.

6. See Walter Benjamin, "The Storyteller: Reflections on the Works of Nicolai Leskov," in *Reflections* (New York: Schoken, 1969).

7. For an interesting portrait of the Peruvian upper class's aspirations in the midcentury, see Alfredo Bryce Echenique, *Un mundo para Julius* (Barcelona: Barral Editores, 1970).

8. See Mario Vargas Llosa, *Contra viento y marea II (1972–1983)* (Barcelona: Seix Barral, 1986), 389; *Contra viento y marea III (1964–1988)* (Barcelona: Seix Barral, 1990), 341, 390.

9. Despite the great divide that exists between Vargas Llosa's neoliberal stance and a marxist position, there are similarities. Like Marx, Vargas Llosa's critique relies heavily on a moral dimension. Marxists have always felt the need to come to terms with their tacit reliance on the traditional values they have been determined to undermine. Over the years such reliance has provided a toehold for nonmarxists who have appropriated marxist methodology as a useful tool. In Latin America some social critics have used the tacit reliance on traditional values to develop their own, often Christian, critique of capitalism, the clearest exemplar being Liberation Theology. Until recently, Vargas Llosa claimed his neoliberal position was grounded on a secular—if not antireligious—worldview. The experience of other neoliberals in the West demonstrates, however, that it is quite difficult for them to maintain their position without eventually availing themselves of an explicit recourse to traditional, i.e., Christian, values. It is not altogether far-fetched to believe that it is only a matter of time before Vargas Llosa embraces the traditional/religious dimension latent in his thinking. See Gustavo Gutierrez, *A Theology of Liberation* (New York: Orbis Books, 1973); Steven Lukes, *Marxism and Morality* (New York: Oxford University Press, 1985); Kai Nielsen, *Marxism and the Moral Point of View: Morality, Ideology, and Historical Materialism* (Boulder, Colo.: Westview Press, 1989); Rodney G. Peffer, *Marxism, Morality, and Social Justice* (Princeton, N.J.: Princeton University Press, 1990).

10. See Vargas Llosa, *Contra viento y marea III*, 309.

11. See Mario Vargas Llosa, "Comedia de equivocaciones," 121, 123.

12. For Marx's classic statement on the matter see his "On the Jewish Question," in *Karl Marx: Early Writings* (New York: McGraw-Hill, 1963).

13. The events were dramatic, and many Peruvians remember them. Alvaro Vargas Llosa, son of Mario Vargas Llosa, recounts the experience: "The situation reached an apotheosis the day the Catholic Church announced that it was going to take in procession the statue of the Señor de los Milagros. This procession usually takes place in October, "the purple month" [when the faithful dress in purple], and only five times in this century had its timing been changed because of special circumstances. The Catholic Church, in an unprecedented action, in the midst of a political battle, took the Señor de los Milagros in procession in May." *El diablo en campaña* (Madrid: Ediciones El País/Aguilar S.A., 1991), 184.

The connections and mutual support between the highest levels of the hierarchy of the Catholic Church and Vargas Llosa were detailed afterward by Vargas Llosa himself in *El pez en el agua*. He tells us, for example, that he was kin to Juan Landázuri Ricketts, archbishop of Peru, who had just retired. His relations with Monsignor Vargas Alzamora, a player in the political game of Peru during this period, are recounted as very sensitive and desperately supportive. In fact, there is an element of intrigue and adventure (one is tempted to say novelistic; involving secret meetings and daring subterfuges) in the attempt of members of the Catholic Church's hierarchy to elect Vargas Llosa president of Peru. See Mario Vargas Llosa, *El pez en el agua: memorias* (Barcelona: Seix Barral, 1993), 484–86.

Of course, his relationship with the hierarchy of the Catholic Church was not altogether smooth. Monsignor José Dammert criticized the attempt to revive what he called "a catholicism of crusade, of conquest, what in Spain used to be called National Catholicism." Vargas Llosa, *El pez en el agua*, 502. But overall, Vargas Llosa the candidate was more than willing to use religion to his advantage. The situation with the Catholic Church was such that Vargas Llosa confesses that "the last thing I imagined was seeing myself changed, from one day to the next, into the defender of the Catholic Church in an electoral contention. That was what began to happen, as soon as the campaign was renewed, when it was evident that, among the elected senators and representatives of Cambio 90 [the opposition] there were at least fifteen Protestant ministers." Mario Vargas Llosa, *El pez en el agua*, 494. His old class and family connections removed the possibility of enacting an alliance with what he might have called the "religious *informales*."

14. See *Partisan Review* 51, no. 3 (1984): 347–55.

15. The image of the Tlamatine and the Amautas as special bearers of culture preceded the arrival of the Spanish in the New World. See, in this connection, Miguel Leon-Portilla, *Aztec Thought and Culture: A Study of the Ancient Nahuatl Mind*, trans. Jack Emory Davis (Norman: University of Oklahoma Press, 1963); Braulio Muñoz, *Sons of the Wind: The Search for Identity in Spanish American Indian Literature* (New Brunswick: Rutgers University Press, 1983).

16. See Vargas Llosa, *El pez en el agua*, 169, 316–17.

17. See Vargas Llosa, *Contra viento y marea III*, 145; *El pez en el agua*, 46.

18. Mario Vargas Llosa has always been suspicious of anything that smacks of atavism or poverty. He is suspicious of the "cultura chicha," for example, a mestizo cultural formation that expanded during the seventies, product of a population that had begun surrounding Lima in the fifties and by the seventies had become strong enough to force the aristocratic classes out of the core of the city and into gated suburbs. See *El pez en el agua*, 536–37.

19. This position is found even in intellectuals who celebrated the rise of a mestizo culture, including the Mexican José Vasconcelos. See Muñoz, *Sons of the Wind*.

20. See Vargas Llosa, *La verdad de las mentiras*, 12; 102–3, 224.

21. See Vargas Llosa, *Contra viento y marea II*, 404.

CHAPTER 5

1. Who is to be considered a Barbarian has changed for Vargas Llosa himself over the years. In his youth he saw capitalists as barbarians and socialists as civilized; he has now reversed the order.

2. *Facundo* was written in 1845. It first appeared in Chile as *Civilización i barbarie: vida de Juan Facundo Quiroga*. The work has gone through several editions. See Domingo Faustino Sarmiento, *Facundo* (Buenos Aires: Editorial Losada, 1942).

3. See Mario Vargas Llosa, *La historia secreta de una novela* (Barcelona: Tusquets, 1971), 9; *El pez en el agua: memorias* (Barcelona: Seix Barral, 1993), 512. For a description of the barbarians in Vargas Llosa's fiction, see *La casa verde* (Barcelona: Seix Barral, 1966), 48; *Historia de Mayta* (Barcelona: Seix Barral, 1984), 211; *La tía Julia y el escribidor* (Barcelona: Seix Barral, 1977), 84; *La guerra del fin del mundo* (Barcelona: Seix Barral, 1981), 451; and *Lituma en los Andes* (Barcelona: Planeta, 1993).

4. In *El pez en el agua*, he describes his encounter with members of the opposition: "Armed with sticks and stones and all kinds of deadly weapons, there came towards me a furious horde of men and women, their faces distorted by hatred, who seemed to emerge from the bowels of time, a prehistory where human beings and animals were indistinguishable, because for both life was a blind struggle to survive. Half naked, with long hair and nails never touched by scissors, surrounded by skeletal children with huge bellies, roaring and vociferating to give each other courage, they hurled themselves against the caravan as if fighting to save their lives or seeking self-immolation, with a temerity and a savagery which showed the inconceivable levels of backwardness into which millions of Peruvians had descended." Vargas Llosa, *El pez en el agua*, 520–21.

5. Vargas Llosa is honest enough to admit that it is hard for him to really understand the poorest masses of Peru. See Mario Vargas Llosa, *El buitre y el ave fenix: conversaciones con Mario Vargas Llosa* (Barcelona: Editorial Anagrama, 1972), 96.

6. See Mario Vargas Llosa, *Contra viento y marea III (1964–1988)* (Barcelona: Seix Barral, 1990), 123–24.

7. Vargas Llosa himself recognizes the differences between Borges's racist ideas and his own. See Mario Vargas Llosa, *Contra viento y marea III*, 475–76.

8. See Mario Vargas Llosa, *Contra viento y marea I (1962–1972)* (Barcelona: Seix Barral, 1983), 212.

9. Earlier in his career Vargas Llosa was willing to side with José María Arguedas in finding some intractable problems in Western culture; problems that other cultures could perhaps help to solve. (See Mario Vargas Llosa, *Contra viento y marea II [1972–1983]* [Barcelona: Seix Barral, 1986], 338–39.) As the years went by and he found a place among the neoliberals, however, he abandoned that position and embraced totally Western culture and the methods to attain it. In this context his disagreement with Günter Grass can be understood. He acknowledges that much barbarism still exists in Peru. But to argue that Peruvians cannot embrace the values of the West (democracy, free market, science) and hence ought to seek other ways of organizing their sociocultural development (perhaps socialism or corporatism) cannot but be conceive as a product of a visceral racism. (See Vargas Llosa, *Contra viento y marea II*, 352.) The best aspect of Latin American reality "undermines that stereotype, deeply ingrained in the Western subconscious, that sees us as barbarous and uncivilized, constitutionally inept for liberty and hence condemned to choose between the model of Pinochet or Fidel Castro." Vargas Llosa, *Contra viento y marea II*, 354. It is ironic that few have contributed more than Vargas Llosa himself to the portrayal of Peru as a land of people incapable of securing freedom and justice.

10. Augusto Salazar Bondy, *Lima la horrible* (México, D.F.: Biblioteca ERA, 1964), 12.

11. Salazar Bondy, *Lima la horrible*, 101.

12. Referring to the limited effort by Gonzales Prada to challenge the colonial mentality, Salazar Bondy notes that even Gonzales Prada's famous disciples (Victor Raúl

Haya de la Torre and José Carlos Mariátegui) were quite unable to change the culture of Peru. That failure, he wrote, "ought to be attributed to the immense corrupting capacity of colonialism, more expert in adorning than in squashing its antibodies." Salazar Bondy, *Lima la horrible*, 126.

13. This was Domingo Faustino Sarmiento's exhortation; but he was not alone in calling for a permanent detour in the development of Latin America. See Braulio Muñoz, *Sons of the Wind: The Search for Indentity in Spanish American Indian Literature* (New Brunswick: Rutgers University Press, 1983).

14. See Vargas Llosa, *Contra viento y marea I*, 119; *Partisan Review* 51, no. 3 (1984): 347–55. For some examples in fiction, see Mario Vargas Llosa, *Conversación en La Catedral* (Barcelona: Seix Barral, 1971), 256. In *Historia de Mayta*, Moises speaks his truth: "it was a good thing for me. I ended up exiled in Paris, was able to finish my thesis and engage in more serious matters." Vargas Llosa, *Historia de Mayta*, 44.

15. See Salazar Bondy, *Lima la horrible*, 100; Vargas Llosa, *Contra viento y marea II*, 345.

16. Leopoldo Zea wrote with much bitterness: "The American has never felt universal. His preoccupation has been, precisely, a preoccupation to incorporate himself into the universal." And the universal, here, means the European. Leopoldo Zea, "Conciencia de las posibilidades del hombre en América," in *La esencia de lo americano* (Buenos Aires: Editorial Pleamar, 1971).

17. This is a long-standing position among the cultural elites of Latin America. (See Muñoz, *Sons of the Wind*.) Vargas Llosa makes the following point as he discusses the work of Juan de Espinosa Medrano, better known as El Lunarejo: "In El Lunarejo one can glimpse at what Peru, Spanish America would be: the southern frontier of the West, a flowering world, unfinished, anxious to find integration, in a hurry and often falling on its face. But the ultimate goal of that obstacle course in which Latin America finds itself is very clear and nothing would help us to attain it more than if the European West understood that our destiny is tied to its own and that the deep desire of our peoples is to achieve prosperous and just societies, within the framework of liberty and coexistence which is the greatest contribution the West has given humanity." *Contra viento y marea III*, 405.

18. It is largely correct to hold that there have never been more than passing attempts by Latin Americans to develop a cultural tradition different from that of the West. Not even the Indigenistas truly believed it was possible to return to the past. It should also be noted that, like most Indigenista writers, Vargas Llosa has always acknowledged that the Western culture was imposed upon the New World. In some of his earlier writings, he even shows resistance to seeing the West as the *non plus ultra* of culture. (See *El buitre y el ave fenix*, 43.) Still, from very early on, he understood that there is no other way for Latin Americans to go on, except by becoming a part of the West. (See *Contra viento y marea III*, 404–5.) By the middle of the eighties, and unlike the Indigenistas who never really came to terms with their hidden desire to eliminate the Indian culture, Vargas Llosa wrote honestly: "Maybe there is no other realist way of integrating our societies than by asking the Indians to pay such a high price; maybe the ideal, that is to say the preservation of the primitive cultures of the Americas, is a utopia which is incompatible with a more urgent one: the establishment of modern societies." *Contra viento y marea III*, 377.

CHAPTER 6

1. This is Quetzalcoatl's vision of Ometeotl, the dual god and fundamental being in Nahuatl cosmology:

And it is stated and said that
Quetzalcoatl called upon, as his
proper god, one who dwells in the
interior of the heaven.

He invoked her, surrounded by a skirt of stars
him who gives light to all things;
Mistress of our flesh, lord of our flesh,
She who clothes herself in black,
He who clothes himself in red,
She who established the earth firmly,
He who gives activity to the earth.

Thither did he direct his words,
thus did he know himself,
toward the place of the duality
and of the nine crossbeams
in which the heaven consists.
And as he knew,
He called on him who dwelled there
directed supplications to him,
living in meditation and in retirement.

In Miguel Leon-Portilla's "Pre-hispanic Thought," in *Major Trends in Mexican Philosophy*, trans. A. Robert Caponigri (Notre Dame: University of Notre Dame Press, 1966), 18.

2. This notion of the present is radicalized in later works. In *Historia de Mayta*, for example, the corruption is so rampant that nothing escapes it. All the "saviors," from the left and the right, are bent on destroying anything of worth. Don Ezequiel, a grocer, says: "They have corrupted everything in Jauja, they have turned even the nuns into prostitutes." Mario Vargas Llosa, *Historia de Mayta* (Barcelona: Seix Barral, 1984), 236. As was already anticipated in *La guerra del fin del mundo*, in this novel Vargas Llosa presents us with a world very much like the Vietnam of the 1960s of the Western imagination: a world engulfed in a total war where old men and old women function as spies, the body count is taken seriously, and even shoe-shine boys are potential terrorists (*Historia de Mayta*, 168). The transportation of the Vietnam experience to Latin America is, expectedly, grafted onto the long-standing distinction between Civilization and Barbarism.

3. Thinking about the Deposito Municipal de Perros, Santiago Savala remembers: "A large field surrounded by an adobe wall the color of shit—the color of Lima, think, the color of Peru." Mario Vargas Llosa, *Conversación en La Catedral* (Barcelona: Seix Barral, 1971), 19. In other novels Vargas Llosa shows us urban individuals mortally afraid or naively mesmerized by the peoples of darkest Peru. They see the Andean region as a barbarous place, good only for exile or lunacy. In turn, for the Andean peoples the coast is

the seat of terror, the command center for the forces of destruction. In *El hablador* we read that, among the Indians, "Saul found spiritual support, stimulation, a justification for life, a compromise, that he did not find in other Peruvian tribes—Jews, Christians, Marxists, etc.—among whom he had lived." Mario Vargas Llosa, *El hablador* (Barcelona: Seix Barral, 1987), 231.

4. In the fictive world of Vargas Llosa, the particular ways in which power is deployed varies from time to time and place to place. The reader has the feeling that power envelops interpersonal relations, weaves itself into religious fervor, suffocates childhood dreams, and undermines the wisdom of old age. As in Michel Foucault's articulation, power appears to be everywhere; it is hence invisible and invincible. This is one reason why some literary critics believe Vargas Llosa to be a postmodern writer. But the insidious ways of power Foucault spoke about apply more squarely to the European experience. Mario Vargas Llosa, on the other hand, writes from and about Peru, a country still struggling to become modern. There power, often naked and triumphant, shows itself in specific, crass ways. In *Conversación en La Catedral*, for example, Don Fermin tells Don Cayo: "With ten million soles there is no coup d'etat that would fail in Peru, Don Cayo." *Conversación en La Catedral*, 425.

5. If in the past there were good Indians and bad landlords, good women and bad men, good proletarians and bad capitalists, now the world is equally neatly divided between victims and victimizers. (Carlos Fuentes makes a similar point with regard to Mexico. In *La muerte de Artemio Cruz,* he classifies Mexicans as either *chingones* or *chingados*.) In Vargas Llosa's fiction, one of the best examples of this manicheistic view is found in *La cuidad y los perros*, where Alberto states: "like it or not, you are a military man here. And what is important in the army is to be a macho, to have steel balls, understand? Eat them or they will eat you, there is no other way. I don't like to be eaten." Mario Vargas Llosa, *La ciudad y los perros* (Barcelona: Seix Barral, 1965), 23. And the Leoncio Prado premilitary academy is a microcosm of Peruvian society.

6. In *La cuidad y los perros* Santiago Savala confesses to Ambrosio, his father's male ex-lover, that life had taught him a hard lesson: he has to play the game as a *vivo*. "'They've sunk me up to my neck, but they're not going to bury me. Do you know why?' says Santiago. 'Because I am going to finish law anyway, Ambrosio.'" Vargas Llosa, *La cuidad y los perros*, 265.

7. One of the clearest examples of this option is found in *Elogio de la madrastra*, where Rigoberto says: "My body is that impossible thing: the egalitarian society" (86). This novel is underrated by literary critics. Rigoberto's withdrawal into a personal world is a statement about the intractability of social problems and the effects they have on individuals; it is the limit-case of an idealist individual crushed by social forces. The retreat is, as all neuroses, an individual and a social symptom. The narrator makes the point, perhaps much too clearly: in his youth, Rigoberto had been "an enthusiastic militant in Accion Católica and had dreamed of changing the world. Soon he realized that, like all collective ideals, that dream was impossible, condemned to failure. His practical spirit spared him from wasting his time fighting battles that sooner or later he would lose. Then he conjectured that maybe the ideal of perfection was possible for the isolated individual, constrained within a limited spatial sphere (personal hygiene or saintliness, for example, or erotic practices) and in time (nocturnal ablutions and amusements before going to sleep)." Mario Vargas Llosa, *Elogio de la madrastra* (Barcelona: Tusquets, 1988), 80.

8. This is most clearly seen in *El hablador*, where Mascarita displaces himself into another world altogether.

9. That there could never be an incorrupt revolutionary is made clear in *Historia de Mayta*. As he listens to Vallejo, a young lieutenant who turns revolutionary and dies at the hands of the police, Mayta thinks, "Why did that young man bring him that nostalgia, that sensation of something definitively extinct? Because he is pure, thought Mayta. He is not corrupted. Politics has not killed his joy for life. He must have never engaged in politics of any type. That is why he is so irresponsible, that is why he says whatever comes to his head" (25–26). Later Moisés, an ex-rebel with a comfortable position, speaks on the matter: "The search for perfection, for the uncorrupted. . . . To pursue purity, in politics, is to reach unreality." Vargas Llosa, *Historia de Mayta*, 52.

10. See Mario Vargas Llosa, *Contra viento y marea I (1962–1972)* (Barcelona: Seix Barral, 1983), 92.

11. He wrote: "They can not talk to us of the 'philosophy of the just' because we all know that behind that hollow phrase hides a contemplative and immobilizing attitude as old as philosophy itself, and whose vacuity becomes apparent as soon as one tries to apply it to a concrete situation." Vargas Llosa, *Contra viento y marea I*, 20.

12. See Mario Vargas Llosa, *Contra viento y marea II (1972–1983)* (Barcelona: Seix Barral, 1986), 437; *La verdad de las mentiras* (Barcelona: Seix Barral, 1990), 128.

13. See *Semana de autor: Mario Vargas Llosa* (Madrid: Ediciones Cultura Hispánica, Instituto de Cooperación Iberoamericana, 1985), 70.

14. See Vargas Llosa, *Contra viento y marea II*, 179, 180; *Contra viento y marea III (1964–1988)* (Barcelona: Seix Barral, 1990), 301.

15. See *Semana de autor*, 56.

16. See Vargas Llosa, *Contra viento y marea II*, 73; *La verdad de las mentiras*, 16, 91, 92.

17. See Vargas Llosa, *Contra viento y marea III*, 497.

18. Following Immanuel Kant and Georg Simmel, Parsons had asked in 1937: if we acknowledge that the social world is shot through with conflict and change, how is order possible? His own solution issued forth as the influential school of structural-functionalism. See Talcott Parsons, *The Structure of Social Action* (New York: Free Press, 1968).

19. See *Semana de autor*, 33.

20. See Vargas Llosa, *Contra viento y marea III*, 491.

21. See Vargas Llosa, *Contra viento y marea III*, 484.

22. Mario Vargas Llosa, "Comedia de equivocaciones," in *América Latina: marca registrada* (Buenos Aires: Grupo Editorial Zeta, S.A., 1992), 12–13.

23. See Vargas Llosa, *Contra viento y marea III*, 490.

24. Mario Vargas Llosa, *El pez en el agua: memorias* (Barcelona: Seix Barral, 1993), 157–58, 363–64.

25. See Vargas Llosa, "Comedia de equivocaciones," 116; *Contra viento y marea II*, 407.

26. See Vargas Llosa, *Contra viento y marea II*, 413.

27. This seems to be why he distanced himself from the likes of Pinochet and Lee Kwan. See Vargas Llosa, *Contra viento y marea III*, 346; "Comedia de equivocaciones," 117; *El pez en el agua*, 265.

28. Vargas Llosa, "Comedia de equivocaciones," 108–9, 117–18.

29. See Vargas Llosa, *El pez en el agua*, 359, 263.

CHAPTER 7

1. See Mario Vargas Llosa, *Contra viento y marea I (1962–1972)* (Barcelona: Seix Barral, 1983), 10.

2. See Mario Vargas Llosa, *Contra viento y marea II (1972–1983)* (Barcelona: Seix Barral, 1986), 74.

3. See Mario Vargas Llosa, *El pez en el agua: memorias* (Barcelona: Seix Barral, 1993), 90.

4. See Mario Vargas Llosa, "Comedia de equivocaciones," in *América Latina: marca registrada* (Buenos Aires: Grupo Editorial Zeta, S.A., 1992), 128.

5. See Vargas Llosa, *El pez en el agua*, 90.

6. See Mario Vargas Llosa, *Contra viento y marea III (1964–1988)* (Barcelona: Seix Barral, 1990), 356.

7. See Vargas Llosa, *El pez en el agua*, 22, 25.

8. See Vargas Llosa, *El pez en el agua*, 505.

9. See Vargas Llosa, *El pez en el agua*, 504–6.

10. See Vargas Llosa, *El pez en el agua*, 508. The political consultant, Mark Malloch Brown, noted after the debacle: "Fujimori became a dark-skinned Peruvian who had taken on the light-skinned and aristocratic Vargas Llosa. He may have been first-generation Peruvian, but in the war of images he represented the polyglot Perú that had been exploited and marginalized by the European interlopers that Vargas Llosa synthesized." Malloch Brown, "The Consultant," in *Granta* 36 (Summer 1991): 93.

11. The rancor against his contender continued well after the defeat. It was particularly visceral among those closest to him. This shows more clearly in Alvaro Vargas Llosa's *El diablo en campaña* (Madrid: Ediciones El País/Aguilar S.A., 1991).

12. Vargas Llosa, *El pez en el agua*, 269.

13. See Vargas Llosa, *El pez en el agua*, 162, 164–65, 173.

14. This strategy was adopted, according to Vargas Llosa's son, following Margaret Thatcher's advice: "In order to withstand the traumas of the first months, advised Thatcher, it is indispensable to surround oneself with a select group of people who think as one does and who would be willing to live with unpopularity. Therein lay, according to her, the key to her own success. . . . The password, then, was to surround oneself with *little Thatchers*." Alvaro Vargas Llosa, *El diablo en campaña*, 27–28.

15. Among his circle of close supporters and advisors he counted such names as Guillermo Van Oordt, Jaime Althaus, Wiltuski, Chersi, Balbi, Jochamonch, Cooper, and Thorndike. Hardly traditional or *cholo* names. The pollster was Mark Malloch Brown, an Englishman who worked for the public relations firm of Sawyer Miller in the United Estates. The political importance of this fact did not escape Malloch Brown, who writes: "The leaders of Mario's crusade to renew Perú sat around a table at our first meeting. Several of them had, like him, spent long periods out of the country: all were visibly upper-class." "The Consultant," 88. John Crabtree writes, more generally: "Fredemo was little more than the political instrument of Peru's socio-economic élite, anxious to regain the political influence it had lost in 1985." *Peru under Garcia: An Opportunity Lost* (Pittsburgh: Pittsburgh University Press, 1992), 180. And, "[t]he problem with Vargas Llosa was that two and a half years later he had already become a figure of the political establishment. By 1990 there was a crisis in the representativeness of the established political par-

ties; a rejection of what they offered by way of alternatives and a search for new political messages and figures; there was a deep fatigue with the *políticos de siempre.*" Crabtree, *Peru Under Garcia*, 181.

16. See Vargas Llosa, *El pez en el agua*, 375.

17. The extent of this feeling of despondency can be seen in his most intimate supporters' reading of the situation; a reading that does not rely on the civilized political theories of Thatcher or Popper but on a *vivo*'s understanding. See Alvaro Vargas Llosa, *El diablo en campaña*, 215.

CHAPTER 8

1. The accusation is not new. It was the staple of liberals and conservatives during the cold war. The accusation worked in large part then because of the pairing of the Soviet Union with Marx's theories. Vargas Llosa follows Karl Popper's critical understanding of the historicism championed by Marxism-Leninism, which claimed that Marx had indeed uncovered the iron laws of history. But Western intellectuals have always known that Marx can also be understood as having a more complex view of the matter: he claimed to have understood the laws of history insofar as he believed them to have made sense of the past. Given his conception of human development in time and his Enlightenment notions of Freedom and Reason, however, he never claimed to know what the future of humanity would be. For him, communism was not to be the end of history. Rather, it is the beginning of *human* history. That is, Marx claimed to have understood the nature of bourgeois society and hence its negation, but that understanding only provided an insight into the next step of historical development. This is why Marx never produced a blueprint of the future society. To have done so would have undercut his deeply held values such as Freedom and Reason. For a detailed analysis of this view, see Braulio Muñoz, *Tensions in Social Theory: Groundwork for a Future Moral Sociology* (Chicago: Loyola University Press, 1993).

2. Following Kant and Hegel, Marx also believed that individual freedom was the goal of history. But what he understood for the Individual and Freedom was different. For Marx, the Individual would become fully developed only in community, not as an egoist participant of the market. Individual Freedom can only be attained within a Just Society. And a Just Society is ruled by Reason, not chance.

3. In discussions of these matters, Vargas Llosa often moves from a philosophical or theoretical to a metaphorical or literary discourse. The presentation of his ideas then takes on a patina of individual taste and preference: "The individual is a product of liberty, like the *Iliad* or *Hamlet*, or like the great scientific discoveries of the modern era. Man differentiates and emancipates himself from the gregarious placenta to which he was tied since the prehistoric times of the horde, and acquires an individual face and a space of his own only in modern times, when the multiplication of activities and uncontrolled economic, social, and artistic functions, in which the spontaneity and fantasy of the individual could be exercised and were needed, stimulated the evolution of philosophical and political thinking until it instituted that notion which breaks free from the historical tradition of humanity: that of individual sovereignty." Mario Vargas Llosa, *Contra viento y marea II (1972–1983)* (Barcelona: Seix Barral, 1986), 434. To have developed the individual, "it is

without doubt the ethical culmination of human history which Benedetto Croce defined, in a suggestive metaphor, as the achievement of liberty." *Contra viento y marea II*, 434–35.

4. See *Semana de autor: Mario Vargas Llosa* (Madrid: Ediciones Cultura Hispánica, Instituto de Cooperación Iberoamericana, 1985), 74.

5. See Mario Vargas Llosa, "Comedia de equivocaciones," in *América Latina: marca registrada* (Buenos Aires: Grupo Editorial Zeta, S.A., 1992), 100.

6. Had he been elected president of Peru, he claims, he would have erased all the economic and political barriers that impede the free collaboration among the Latin American countries. See Mario Vargas Llosa, *El pez en el agua: memorias* (Barcelona: Seix Barral, 1993), 433–34; *Contra viento y marea II*, 140–42.

7. Vargas Llosa has been quite self-conscious regarding his relation with the Cuban revolution. In December of 1974 he wrote in *Plural*, Mexico: "Our adhesion to the revolution was unlimited and intractable, almost religious." *Contra viento y marea I (1962–1972)* (Barcelona: Seix Barral, 1993), 288. And "Cuba signified for me the first tangible proof that socialism could be a reality in our countries, and, above all, the first proof that socialism could be, at the same time a just redistribution of wealth and the installation of a human social system, as well as a regimen compatible with liberty." *Contra viento y marea I*, 298. "That is why, despite the biological horror produced in me by police-based societies and dogmatism, those systems of only one truth, if I have to choose between the two, I clench my teeth and continue to say 'for socialism.'" *Contra viento y marea I*, 299.

8. See Mario Vargas Llosa, "Taking a Stand," trans. E. Watson, *The Massachusetts Review* 27 (1986): 514–21.

9. See Vargas Llosa, *El pez en el agua*, 307, 314–15.

10. See Vargas Llosa, "Taking a Stand," 515, 520.

11. The point was made earlier by Augusto Salazar Bondy: "In short, the reconciliation of antagonistic positions, plus the repertoire of glibness, reveals to us a content with an inherent bind: to prevent protest, to cut the rebellion and creative violence of the masses before they are born." *Lima la horrible* (México, D.F.: Biblioteca ERA, 1964), 96. See also Vargas Llosa, *El pez en el agua*, 301.

12. See Vargas Llosa, *El pez en el agua*, 310, 143, 148.

CHAPTER 9

1. A Tasurinchi reflects: "How miserable life must be for those who do not have, as we do, people who speak, he reflected. Thanks to what you tell us, it is as if what has happened would happen again and again." Mario Vargas Llosa, *El hablador* (Barcelona: Seix Barral, 1987), 60. And the narrator expands: "I have the impression that the storyteller does not only bring current news. Also the past. It is probable that he is, at the same time, the memory of the community. That he fulfills a function similar to the troubadours and jugglers of the Middle Ages." *El hablador*, 91.

2. One of the characters in Vargas Llosa's *La guerra del fin del mundo*, a novel that sharply contrasts Civilization and Barbarism, posits that the only way to preserve the past is to write it down. *La guerra del fin del mundo* (Barcelona: Seix Barral, 1981), 341. This

idea is central to Vargas Llosa's fiction. The majority of his most interesting characters are either writers or journalists. In fact, he seems so obsessed with the role of the writer, his reflection on the process of writing so suffuses his critical and fictive works, that his ruminations on the matter sometimes border on being narcissistic and incestuous.

3. Well before the Spanish conquerors set down the vision of America in their feverish—half description, half confession—chronicles, Vargas Llosa notes, the Incas had practiced official deception: "Five centuries before the Soviet's *Great Encyclopedia* and George Orwell's *1984*, the Incas practiced the manipulation of the past in view of present political expediences. Each Inca emperor ascended to the throne with a coterie of *amautas* or wise men in charge of rectifying history in order to show that it reached its full development with the rule of the current Inca, to whom was attributed the great deeds of his predecessors." Mario Vargas Llosa, *Contra viento y marea III (1964–1988)* (Barcelona: Seix Barral, 1990), 231–32. Vargas Llosa underscores a truism: the feat has been accomplished by ruling powers all over the world including, of course, the West from the Greeks to the American government.

4. Quoted by Michael Palencia-Roth, "The Art of Memory in García Márquez and Vargas Llosa," *MLN* 105, no. 2 (March 1990): 357.

5. One of the clearest exemplars of biographical inscription is the novel *La tía Julia*, which is largely based on the author's courtship and marriage to his aunt. More generally, it has been noted that the action of *La Casa Verde* takes place between 1920 and 1960, a time when many conflicts and exploitation of the Amazonian Indians took place. During the Oncenio (1919–30) the atrocities in that region reached very high proportions. The novel records some of the abuses. See Marvin A. Lewis, *From Lima to Leticia: The Peruvian Novels of Mario Vargas Llosa* (Lanham, Md.: University Press of America, 1983), 105–6. In the same novel, Vargas Llosa's attention to the presence of Sánchez Cerro (an army officer who deposed the then Peruvian president, Augusto B. Leguia) in national politics records the authoritarian tendencies among northern Peruvians. In *La guerra del fin del mundo*, he weaves freely fictional and historical characters: the myopic, asthmatic newspaper reporter is clearly modeled after Euclides da Cunha, and Galileo Gall represents the Scottish anarchist, Cunninghame Graham. Kovács notes, in the case of *Pantaleón y las visitadoras*, "Although the figure of Captain Pantoja is an invention of Vargas Llosa's, the story itself is based upon a real situation which developed in the Amazon region of Peru in the 1950's." See Katherine S. Kovács, "The Bureaucratization of Knowledge and Sex in Flaubert and Vargas Llosa," *Comparative Literature Studies* 5 (Spring 1984): 43. For further examples of such historical events in Varga Llosa's work, see José Miguel Oviedo, *Mario Vargas Llosa: La invención de una realidad* (Barcelona: Seix Barral, 1982).

6. Recently, Vargas Llosa has followed Camus in believing that the human predicament cannot be explained by history alone: "I think that Camus was very lucid with regard to two things: the first was that history is not everything. That is, to try to explain human predicaments exclusively by means of history is insufficient: man is not only history but something more. The purely historic vision of reality and of human problems is incomplete and always leads one to incomplete solutions to those problems. The second is the danger of ideology. I think that in this matter Camus was extraordinarily lucid. The danger of a purely intellectual, abstract vision must cut reality down so it will fit into its patterns. But reality is always more complex, richer. The only way in which you can impose

a pattern on a reality that rejects it is through violence." Interview with Ignacio Solares, *Partisan Review* 51, no. 3 (1984): 347–55. That "something more" is not accessible through the scientific recording method but through art. See also Mario Vargas Llosa, *El buitre y el ave fenix: conversaciones con Mario Vargas Llosa*, (Barcelona: Editorial Anagrama, 1972), 38.

7. Sometimes the aesthetic daemon might need a hand: Michael Palencia-Roth writes with regard to Vargas Llosa's tumultuous relationship with his aunt and ex-wife: "That Vargas Llosa tried to prevent publication of *Lo que Varguitas no dijo* and also tried to buy up all available copies indicates that he preferred his own version to be the only one in the minds of his readers." "The Art of Memory in García Márquez and Vargas Llosa," 356.

CHAPTER 10

1. See Mario Vargas Llosa, *El pez en el agua: memorias* (Barcelona: Seix Barral, 1993), 11–14.

2. In a very public controversy with Angel Rama, Vargas Llosa showed himself quite sensitive to being addressed by his full name. Angel Rama chastised him for appearing to claim a special social status for himself. This fact was used against Vargas Llosa by the Fujimori forces during the political campaign for the presidency of Peru. In general, it seems, Peruvians are not fond of suffering the pretensions of upper-class members.

3. This is clear in the most trivial of acts, such as the manner of kissing. He recounts his experiences with his Aunt Julia: "She rewarded me with a kiss. Not a 'tongue kiss': we had had a discussion about this among the neighborhood kids and I had defended the thesis that one could not 'tongue kiss' one's sweetheart; that was done only with the party girls, the *huachafitas*, the poor mestizas. To 'tongue kiss' was like pawing, and who but the worst of degenerates would paw a decent girl?" Vargas Llosa, *El pez en el agua*, 77.

4. See Vargas Llosa, *El pez en el agua*, 54, 76.

5. He writes about his return to Miraflores: "It was very emotional to see my aunt and uncle and to be in such a beautiful neighborhood, with tree-lined streets and little houses with manicured gardens. Above all, it was wonderful to feel I was once again with my family, far from that man, and to know that I would never have to hear or see him or be afraid again. The house of Uncle Jorge and Aunt Gaby, who had two small children, Silvia and Jorgito, was very small, but they accommodated us somehow—I slept on a couch—and my happiness was unlimited." Vargas Llosa, *El pez en el agua*, 59.

6. See Vargas Llosa, *El pez en el agua*, 53.

7. See Vargas Llosa, *El pez en el agua*, 101.

8. See Mario Vargas Llosa, *Contra viento y marea III (1964–1988)* (Barcelona: Seix Barral, 1990), 238.

9. See Mario Vargas Llosa, *Contra viento y marea II (1972–1983)* (Barcelona: Seix Barral, 1986), 71, 214; *Contra viento y marea III*, 240.

10. See Vargas Llosa, *Contra viento y marea III*, 243–44; *El pez en el agua*, 291.

11. See Mario Vargas Llosa, *La orgía perpetua: Flaubert y "Madame Bovary,"* (Madrid: Ediciones Taurus, 1975), 103–4.

12. See Mario Vargas Llosa, *El buitre y el ave fenix: conversaciones con Mario Varga Llosa* (Barcelona: Editorial Anagrama, 1972), 65.

13. It is interesting to note that, according to Vargas Llosa, there have been other scandals in his family. His Uncle Lucho, for example, got one of his cousins pregnant just before he went to the university. Vargas Llosa married his own cousin, Patricia, years later. *El pez en el agua*, 183.

14. In his influential essay on García Márquez he wrote: "He who uses all of human reality as a resource for such an egoist and demented aim (to rival God) can only achieve his goal by serving his vocation with a similar madness and egoism." Mario Vargas Llosa, *García Márquez: historia de un deicidio* (Barcelona: Barral Editores, 1971), 210.

15. "He who fails, decided to fail; he who succeeds, wanted to succeed," he noted in 1975. See Vargas Llosa, *García Márquez: historia de un deicidio*, 209. As we have seen, this attitude, developed in the context of art, would eventually become crucial for his defense of a free market economy.

16. Vargas Llosa, *El pez en el agua*, 33.

17. See Mario Vargas Llosa, *Contra viento y marea I (1962–1972)* (Barcelona: Seix Barral, 1983), 114.

18. See Mario Vargas Llosa, *El hablador* (Barcelona: Seix Barral, 1987), 159.

19. See Juan Biondi and Eduardo Zapata, *Representación oral en las calles de Lima* (Lima: Universidad de Lima, 1994); Juan Biondi and Eduardo Zapata, *Voz, mujer y violencia sexual en las calles de Lima* (Lima: Instituto de diálogo y Propuestas, 1996).

20. He wrote earlier in his career: "I only write about Peru and am only interested in writing about Peru." Quoted by José Miguel Oviedo, *Mario Vargas Llosa: la invención de una realidad* (Barcelona: Seix Barral, 1982), 32.

21. See Vargas Llosa, *Contra viento y marea II*, 240; *García Márquez: historia de un deicidio*, 95; *La verdad de las mentiras* (Barcelona: Seix Barral, 1990), 103–4, 191.

22. See Alvaro Vargas Llosa, *El diablo en campaña* (Madrid: Ediciones El País/Aguilar, S.A., 1991), 139.

23. See Vargas Llosa, *Contra viento y marea II*, 415–16; *El pez en el agua*, 312–13.

CHAPTER 11

1. See Cesar Vallejo, *Poemas Humanos: A Bilingual Edition*, trans. Clayton Eshleman (New York: Grove Press, 1968).

2. Vargas Llosa follows the Peruvian historian Jorge Basadre, who reflected on the question of Peruvian identity for most of his life. See Jorge Basadre, *Perú: problema y posibilidad. Ensayo de una síntesis de la evolución histórica del Perú* (Lima: Biblioteca Peruana/Librería Francesa Científica/Casa Editorial E. Rosay, 1931); *Meditaciones sobre el destino histórico del Perú* (Lima: Ediciones Huascarán, 1947); *La promesa de la vida peruana y otros ensayos* (Lima: Editorial Juan Mejía Baca, 1958).

3. See Jorge Luis Borges, "Borges and I," in *Labyrinths: Selected Stories and Other Writings* (New York: New Directions, 1964).

4. See Mario Vargas Llosa, *La utopía arcaica: José María Arguedas y las ficciones del indigenismo* (Mexico, D.F.: Fondo de Cultura Económica, 1996); Braulio Muñoz, "José María Arguedas: Indian of the Heart," *Americas* (May–June, 1982), trans. into Spanish as "José María Arguedas: Indio de Corazón," *Américas* (May–June, 1982); Braulio Muñoz,

Sons of the Wind: The Search for Identity in Spanish American Indian Literature (New Brunswick: Rutgers University Press, 1983).

5. See Vargas Llosa, *La utopía arcaica*, 90–91.

6. See Varga Llosa, *La utopía arcaica*, 94–95.

7. For Vargas Llosa's discussion of the role of literature and the writer in relation to José María Arguedas, see particularly the first chapter of *La utopía arcaica*.

8. See Muñoz, *Sons of the Wind*.

9. Miguel Angel Asturias (Nobel Prize, 1967) wrote two novels that deal directly with these issues: *Hombres de maíz* (Buenos Aires: Editorial Losada, 1966), and *Mulata de tal* (Buenos Aires: Editorial Losada, 1963).

10. See Vargas Llosa, *La utopía arcaica*, 333.

11. For Vargas Llosa's account of Arguedas's fascination with violence, see *La utopía arcaica*, 86–87.

12. See Ferdinand Tönnies, *Community and Association (Gemeinschaft und Gesellschaft)*, trans. and supplemented by Charles P. Loomis (London: Routledge & Kegan Paul, 1974).

13. See Émile Durkheim, *The Division of Labor in Society*, trans. George Simpson (New York: Free Press, 1964).

14 See Vargas Llosa, *La utopía arcaica*, 257, 259. The disagreement between himself and Arguedas is conclusive, as far as Vargas Llosa is concerned. For Arguedas the coast is bad and the highland good, the foreigner is bad and the native good, society is bad and community good. For Vargas Llosa the valuation is simply reversed. See *La utopía arcaica*, 260, 271.

15. Vargas Llosa writes: "Except in a symbolic and administrative sense—that is, the most precarious sense—'the Peruvian' does not exist. There only exist Peruvians, a fan of races, cultures, languages, standards of living, behaviors and customs, more dissimilar than similar to one another, whose common denominator is reduced, in most cases, to living in the same territory and under the same authority." *La utopía arcaica*, 210.

16. Vargas Llosa follows Basadre's lead on this point. See *La utopía arcaica*, 203.

17. *Pendejo* may be translated as a foolhardy coward.

18. See *La utopía arcaica*, 273.

Selected Bibliography

América Latina: marca registrada. Buenos Aires: Grupo Editorial Zeta, S.A., 1992.

Asturias, Miguel Angel. *Hombres de maíz.* Buenos Aires: Editorial Losada, 1966.

———. *Mulata de tal.* Buenos Aires: Editorial Losada, 1963.

Basadre, Jorge. *La promesa de la vida peruana y otros ensayos.* Lima: Editorial Juan Mejía Baca, 1958.

———. *Meditaciones sobre el destino histórico del Perú.* Lima: Ediciones Huascarán, 1947.

———. *Perú: problema y posibilidad. Ensayo de una síntesis de la evolución histórica del Perú.* Lima: Biblioteca Peruana/Librería Francesa Científica/Casa Editorial E. Rosay, 1931.

Benjamin, Walter. *Illuminations.* New York: Schoken, 1969.

Berlin, Isaiah. *The Hedgehog and the Fox: An Essay on Tolstoy's View of History.* London: Weindenfeld & Nicolson, 1953.

———. *Four Essays on Liberty.* Oxford: Oxford University Press, 1969.

Biondi, Juan, and Eduardo Zapata. *Representación oral en las calles de Lima.* Lima: Universidad de Lima, 1994.

———. *Voz, mujer y violencia sexual en las calles de Lima.* Lima: Instituto de Diálogo y Propuestas, 1996.

Borges, Jorge Luís. *Labyrinths: Selected Stories and Other Writings.* New York: New Directions, 1964.

Collasos, Oscar, Julio Cortázar, and Mario Vargas Llosa. *Literatura en la revolución y revolución en la literatura.* México, D.F.: Siglo Veintiuno, 1976.

Crabtree, John. *Peru under Garcia: An Opportunity Lost.* Pittsburgh: Pittsburgh University Press, 1992.

Danto, Arthur Coleman. *After the End of Art: Contemporary Art and the Pale of History.* Princeton: Princeton University Press, 1997.

Donoso, José. *The Boom in Spanish American Literature : A Personal History.* Trans. Gregory Kolovakos. New York: Columbia University Press, 1977.

Durkheim, Émile. *The Division of Labor in Society.* Trans. George Simpson. New York: Free Press, 1964.

Echenique, Alfredo Bryce. *Un mundo para Julius.* Barcelona: Barral Editores, 1970.

Espejo de escritores: entrevistas con Borges, Cortazar, Fuentes, Goytisolo, Onetti, Puig, Rama, Rulfo, Sanchez, Vargas Llosa. Notas y prólogo de Reina Roffe. Hanover: Ediciones del Norte, 1985.

Foucault, Michel. *The Order of Things: An Archaeology of the Human Sciences.* New York: Vintage Books, 1970.

Fuentes, Carlos. *La muerte de Artemio Cruz.* Mexico, D. F.: Fondo de Cultura Económica, 1975.

Gadamer, Hans-Georg. *Truth and Method.* New York: Seabury Press, 1975.

Goldmann, Lucién. *Le dieu cache: étude sur la vision tragique dans les Pensées de Pascal et dans le théâtre de Racine.* Paris: Gallimard, 1955.

Gutierrez, Gustavo. *A Theology of Liberation.* Ed. and trans. Sister Caridad Inda and John Eagleson. New York: Orbis Books, 1973.

Habermas, Jürgen. *Legitimation Crisis.* Boston: Beacon Press, 1973.

———. *Twelve Lectures on Modernity.* Cambridge: MIT Press, 1990.

Kant, Immanuel. *Critique of Judgment.* New York: Hafner, 1951.

Lang, Berel, ed. *The Death of Art,* New York: Haven Publications, 1984.

Leon-Portilla, Miguel. *Aztec Thought and Culture: A Study of the Ancient Nahuatl Mind.* Trans. Jack Emory Davis. Norman: University of Oklahoma Press, 1963.

Lewis, Marvin A. *From Lima to Leticia: The Peruvian Novels of Mario Vargas Llosa.* Lanham, Md.: University Press of America, 1983.

Lippy, Charles H. *Modern American Popular Religion: A Critical Assessment and Annotated Bibliography.* Westport, Conn.: Greenwood Press, 1996.

Lukacs, Georg. *The Theory of the Novel: A Historico-Philosophical Essay on the Forms of Great Epic Literature.* Cambridge: MIT Press, 1968.

Lukes, Steven. *Marxism and Morality.* New York: Oxford University Press, 1985.

Marty, Martin E., and R. Scott Appleby, eds. *Fundamentalisms and Society: Reclaiming the Sciences, the Family, and Education.* Chicago: University of Chicago Press, 1993.

Marx, Karl. *Karl Marx: Early Writings.* New York: McGraw-Hill, 1963.

Memmi, Albert. *The Colonizer and the Colonized.* Boston: Beacon Press, 1965.

Merton, Robert K. *Science, Technology and Society in Seventeenth Century England.* New York: H. Fertig, 1970.

———. *The Sociology of Science: Theoretical and Empirical Investigations.* Ed. and with an introduction by Norman W. Storer. Chicago: University of Chicago Press, 1973.

Meyer, Enrique. "Peru in Deep Trouble: Mario Vargas Llosa's Inquest in the Andes' Reexamined." *Cultural Anthropology* 6, no. 4 (1991).

Muñoz, Braulio. "Law-Givers: From Plato to Freud and Beyond." *Theory, Culture and Society* 6 (1989).

———. "On Relativity, Relativism, and Social Theory." *Rationality, Relativism and the Human Sciences.* Ed. Joseph Margolis, Michael Krausz, and R. M. Burian. Dordrecht, Netherlands: Martinus Nijhoff Publishers, 1986.

———. *Sons of the Wind: The Search for Identity in Spanish American Indian Literature.* New Brunswick: Rutgers University Press, 1983. Translated as *Huairapamushcas: la búsqueda de la identidad en la novela indigenista hispanoamericana.* With a new introduction. Trans. Nancy K. Muñoz. Temuco: Ediciones de la Universidad de la Frontera, 1996.

———. *Tensions in Social Theory: Groundwork for a Future Moral Sociology.* Chicago: Loyola University Press, 1993.

Nielsen, Kai. *Marxism and the Moral Point of View: Morality, Ideology, and Historical Materialism.* Boulder, Colo.: Westview Press, 1989.

Nietzsche, Friedrich. *Beyond Good and Evil: Prelude to a Philosophy of the Future.* New York: Vintage Books, 1966.

Oviedo, Jose Miguel. *Mario Vargas Llosa: la invención de una realidad.* Barcelona: Seix Barral, 1982.

Parsons, Talcott. *The Structure of Social Action.* New York: Free Press, 1937.

Paz, Octavio. *El arco y la lira.* México, D.F.: Fondo de Cultura Económica, 1956.

——. *El laberinto de la soledad*. México, D.F.: Fondo de Cultura Económica, 1963.
Peffer, Rodney G. *Marxism, Morality, and Social Justice*. Princeton, N.J.: Princeton University Press, 1990.
Plato. *The Republic of Plato*. Trans. with notes and interpretive essay by Allan Bloom. New York: Basic Books, 1968.
Popper, Karl R. *The Open Society and Its Enemies*. Vols. 1 and 2. Princeton: Princeton University Press, 1962.
Rama, Angel, and Mario Vargas Llosa. *García Marquéz y la problemática de la novela*. Buenos Aires: Ediciones Corregidor, 1973.
Rieff, Philip. *Freud: The Mind of the Moralist*. Chicago: University of Chicago Press, 1959.
Salazar Bondy, Augusto. *Lima la horrible*. México, D.F.: Biblioteca ERA, 1964.
Sarmiento, Domingo Faustino. *Facundo*. Buenos Aires: Editorial Losada, 1942.
Semana de autor: Mario Vargas Llosa. Madrid: Ediciones Cultura Hispánica, Instituto de Cooperación Iberoamericana, 1985.
Tönnies, Ferdinand. *Community and Association (Gemeinschaft und Gesellschaft)*. Trans. and supplemented by Charles P. Loomis. London: Routledge & Kegan Paul, 1974.
Urquide, Julia. *My Life with Mario Vargas Llosa*. Trans. C. R. Perricone and Peter Lang. New York: American Studies Press, 1988.
Valdez Moses, Michael. *The Novel and the Globalization of Culture*. Oxford: Oxford University Press. 1995.
Vargas Llosa, Alvaro. *El diablo en campaña*. Madrid: Ediciones El País/Aguilar S.A., 1991.
Watts, Ian. *The Rise of the Novel: Studies in DeFoe, Richardson, and Fielding*. Berkeley: University of California Press, 1957.
Weber, Max. *The Protestant Ethic and the Spirit of Capitalism*. New York : Charles Scribner's Sons, 1958.
Zea, Leopoldo. *La esencia de lo americano*. Buenos Aires: Editorial Pleamar, 1971.

NOVELS BY MARIO VARGAS LLOSA

La ciudad y los perros [The Time of the Hero]. Barcelona: Seix Barral, 1965.
La casa verde [The Green House]. Barcelona: Seix Barral,1966.
Conversación en La Catedral [Conversation in The Cathedral] Barcelona: Seix Barral, 1971.
Pantaleón y las visitadoras [Captain Pantoja and the Special Service]. Barcelona: Seix Barral, 1976.
La tía Julia y el escribidor [Aunt Julia and the Scriptwriter]. Barcelona: Seix Barral, 1977.
La guerra del fin del mundo [The War of the End of the World]. Barcelona: Seix Barral, 1981.
Historia de Mayta [The Real Life of Alejandro Mayta]. Barcelona: Seix Barral, 1984.
¿Quién mató a Palomino Molero [Who Killed Palomino Molero?]*?* Barcelona: Seix Barral, 1986.
El hablador [The Storyteller]. Barcelona: Seix Barral, 1987.
Elogio de la madrastra [In praise of the Stepmother]. Barcelona: Tusquets, 1988.
Lituma en los Andes [Death in the Andes]. Barcelona: Planeta, 1993.
Los cuadernos de don Rigoberto [The Notebooks of Don Rigoberto]. Madrid: Alfaguara/ Peisa, 1997.

SELECTED CRITICAL WORKS BY MARIO VARGAS LLOSA

García Márquez: historia de un deicidio. Barcelona: Barral Editores, 1971.

La orgía perpetua: *Flaubert y "Madame Bovary."* Madrid: Taurus, 1975.

Contra viento y marea I (1962–1972). Barcelona: Seix Barral, 1983.

Contra viento y marea II (1972–1983). Barcelona: Seix Barral, 1986.

Contra viento y marea III (1964–1988). Barcelona: Seix Barral, 1990.

La verdad de las mentiras. Barcelona: Seix Barral, 1990.

El pez en el agua: memorias. Barcelona: Seix Barral, 1993.

Desafíos a la libertad. Madrid: El País/Aguilar, 1994.

La utopía arcaica: José María Arguedas y las ficciones del indigenismo, México, D.F.: Fondo de Cultura Económica, 1996.

Index

About the Author

Braulio Muñoz was born in Peru. He holds a Ph.D. in sociology from the University of Pennsylvania. Professor Muñoz has lectured and written extensively on such topics as psychoanalysis, social and critical theory, and cultural identity. His major works include *Sons of the Wind: The Search for Identity in Spanish American Indian Literature* (Rutgers University Press) and *Tensions in Social Theory: Groundwork for a Future Moral Sociology* (Loyola University Press). Muñoz chairs the department of Sociology and Anthropology at Swarthmore College and is currently working on a manuscript on the nonrational dimensions of modern life.